PIRATES OF THE DELAWARE

"I'M THE CAPTAIN OF THIS SHIP, AND IF ANY MAN DARES TO QUESTION THAT,
I'LL DEAL WITH HIM".

PIRATES OF THE DELAWARE

Rupert Sargent Holland

WITH ILLUSTRATIONS BY
W. H. WOLF

4880 Lower Valley Road, Atglen, PA 19310 USA

This book is a faithful reprint of a novel first released in 1925. Written by Rupert Sargent Holland, and illustrated by W. H. Wolf.

Published by Schiffer Publishing Ltd.
4880 Lower Valley Road
Atglen, PA 19310
Phone: (610) 593-1777; Fax: (610) 593-2002
E-mail: Info@schifferbooks.com

For the largest selection of fine reference books on this and related subjects, please visit our web site at **www.schifferbooks.com**
We are always looking for people to write books on new and related subjects. If you have an idea for a book please contact us at the above address.

This book may be purchased from the publisher.
Include $3.95 for shipping.
Please try your bookstore first.
You may write for a free catalog.

In Europe, Schiffer books are distributed by:
Bushwood Books
6 Marksbury Ave.
Kew Gardens
Surrey TW9 4JF
England
Phone: 44 (0)208 392-8585
Fax: 44 (0)208 392-9876
E-mail: Info@bushwoodbooks.co.uk
Website: www.bushwoodbooks.co.uk
Free postage in the UK. Europe: air mail at cost.
Try your bookstore first.

Designed by "Sue"
Type set in New Baskerville BT

ISBN: 0-7643-2487-X
Printed in China

CONTENTS

ILLUSTRATIONS

PIRATES OF THE DELAWARE

I

JARED LEE

It was May, and the leaves of the spreading maple outside the southern window of Mr. Nathaniel Carroll's law office were a rich, lustrous green. The air was soft, and had a spicy scent, as if it had blown over gardens of clove pinks. Altogether it was an afternoon made for anything but poring over legal papers, browsing in dusty quartos, or writing out interminable deeds, compounded largely of "whereas" and "therefore."

So thought Jared Lee, as he sat at his table, drawn up close to the southern window, and gazed out at the pedestrians, more fortunate than he, who strolled under the shade trees that lined Prune Street. He had the room to himself, for Mr. Carroll was still enjoying the hearty dinner he partook of with his family in his residence next door. He would come in presently, full of good food and importance, and treat Jared to a moral discourse, interlarded with Latin maxims, before he settled down to his

9

post-prandial consideration of the affairs of the various worthy Philadelphians who were his clients.

But Mr. Carroll was sixty and Jared was twenty, and Mr. Carroll's desire was all for law and order, while Jared craved adventure. Possibly in time Jared might grow to be like his preceptor, but he doubted it. Only a sense of loyalty to his father, who was so eager for him to be a lawyer, had kept him in the office the past winter, instead of returning to his home at Lancaster or striking out for himself, to see a bit of the world.

There were, of course, many more interesting people in Philadelphia than in Lancaster, which was a small country town, parties were much more elegant and luxurious, and the talk in the taverns and coffee-houses was much more spirited and entertaining. That group of merry blades who met at the City Tavern, for instance! There were no young fellows like them to be found in Lancaster. More particularly none like Hal Norroy......

Jared leaned forward, gazing out into Prune Street. A young man was strolling in his direction, a tall and slender figure, very exquisite in his long-tailed, short-waisted coat of changeable plum-colored silk, his light yellow nankeen breeches and lilac and white striped stockings. His high-crowned hat of felt was set at just a suspicion of an angle on his handsome head.

Jared whistled through the open window. The young man caught the sound, looked up, and left the footway for Mr. Carroll's lawn. There was an amiable smile on his fresh-colored face as he stopped outside the window. "Mole," he jeered; "bookworm, mouse!"

Jared acknowledged the appellations with an amused chuckle. "Peacock, turkey cock, rooster!" he retaliated. "Magnificent Master Norroy!"

"So Jared Lee is busy with his studies, is he? Tell me, have you learned the rule of three yet?"

"I can draw up a writ that will clap a malefactor into jail."

"Are you a malefactor then, that you have to stay in that prison?"

Jared made a grimace. "If I stay here long enough I may become a respectable citizen, a 'pillar of society,' as Mr. Carroll says."

"Ah, that's a dignity I've never aspired to. I was born respectable, but I've been shedding the garments ever since; I got rid of the last one on the Michaelmas Eve before I left England."

"How long ago was that?"

Norroy laid his polished malacca walking-stick on the window-ledge and clasped his hands over it. "Dates always confuse me. I leave them to scriveners. However, I will make an effort. Let me see. This is the year 1793, isn't it? I left the realm of

His Gracious Majesty King George the Third in
1791, two years ago. And I have no doubt that
His Majesty has been graciously pleased to miss me."

Jared smiled. He had heard all manner of stories
of this amusing young man, but had never before had
the opportunity to question him directly. "Is it
true you are an English nobleman?" he asked.
" And that your right title is Lord Norroy?"

"Master Lee, do you think you have me in the
witness-box, that you dare to ask me such personal
questions?"

"Oh, I beg your pardon!"

The other made a gesture. "You are forgiven, my
boy. Whatever I may have been in England, I am
plain Henry Norroy here, called by my friends Hal."

This was practically an admission, it seemed to
Jared, that the fresh-colored gentleman with the
reddish-brown hair had been a nobleman in England.
He would have liked extremely to know what it was
that Norroy had done on the Michaelmas Eve he
had referred to, but he sensed that Norroy was not
a man to be questioned against his will.

" 'Tis a wonderfully fine afternoon," said Norroy.
" If you and I were to stroll down High Street
we might gladden the eyes of many pretty ladies."

"I have no doubt of it. But it wouldn't gladden
Mr. Carroll to find his student missing. There are
times when, in spite of my very evident devotion to

the law, he gives me the impression that he thinks me inclined to be frivolous."

"You frivolous! I had thought the worthy Mr. Carroll more discerning."

"He is not too well disposed toward frequenters of taverns."

"But surely the gentleman knows there is more of human nature to be learned over a tavern table than in all the law courts in the world! And when it comes to actual information of what is going on in the neighborhood—" Norroy shrugged his shoulders and gestured with his hands.

"I have pointed that out to him," said Jared. "I told him only this morning some of the gossip I'd picked up at the City Tavern concerning the highwayman on the Chester Road. He listened politely enough, and then told me that it took long experience to be able to winnow what was truth from what was fancy in the stories of witnesses. 'In a coffeehouse,' said he, 'every man likes to draw the long bow; but if we were to believe everything we hear in such places, we would conclude there was no man who was not a criminal.'"

" Sapient indeed!" declared Norroy. " And I presume your response was, 'Worthy master, do you believe there has ever been a man who was not at some time if not a criminal, at least criminally inclined?'"

Jared laughed. "Why no, I didn't say that. Mr. Carroll doesn't take over-kindly to argument; it interrupts the flow of his discourse."

"I see. He likes to pour his wisdom into the ear of such a patient vessel as Jared Lee. On my word, I don't see how you manage to stomach it!"

"Nor I, at times. Sometimes I hate the whole business! This afternoon, for example. What am I doing here, cooped up like some sort of fowl, when I might be seeing the world and making my fortune?"

"A question that has presented itself to me on several occasions in my own career," Norroy observed. He removed his high felt hat and touched his forehead with a cambric handkerchief. "Usually the question occurs on a fine day of spring or early summer. Some men find the answer in taking physic, some in running away. I prefer the latter course myself."

"A man like you would!" said Jared, admiringly.

Norroy held up his hand with the handkerchief. "Now don't you take me as a pattern! I've sins enough on my conscience without adding that of holding myself out as a model for a well brought up lad to follow. I've no doubt the worthy Mr. Carroll would advocate the taking of physic, as presumably he frequently did himself on spring days in his wild youth."

"He never had a wild youth," Jared retorted.

"Don't be too sure about that. Listen to his stories the next time he invites you to one of his supper parties, when the ladies have withdrawn, and he sits with his cronies over the Madeira and walnuts. *In vino veritas;* the truth lies in the wine cup."

"Then you think I should stay here, and continue to puzzle my wits over deeds and writs and the study of easements, rights, and incorporeal hereditaments?" said Jared, in a disappointed tone.

"I decline to be your adviser," answered Norroy, replacing his hat and taking his malacca stick from the window-ledge. He added with a smile, "There is this at least to be said for the study of the law: It instructs the student how he may steer clear of paying the penalties for his misdemeanors. That also I daresay the worthy Mr. Carroll would admit over his third glass of port."

With that the plum-coated gentleman turned and surveyed the thoroughfare, while he twirled his walking-stick lightly in his fingers. "Mayhap I will see you tonight at the tavern; meantime, as I have observed, there are pretty eyes on High Street for me to gladden. And speaking of that, here's a lady in a chaise who looks as if she desired to make my acquaintance."

A chaise had indeed stopped opposite the maple tree, and a young woman was glancing in Norroy's direction. That gentleman, agile and graceful, quickly stepped out to the road. He raised his hat. "At your service, madame."

Jared didn't hear what she answered. His attention had suddenly been caught by the sight of a man who had just come around the corner of a house on Fourth Street and who was staring intently at the lady in the carriage. He was a thickset man in brown, a rough-looking customer. Then Jared saw the driver of the chaise, an elderly man in a snuff-colored suit, turn his head and catch sight of the stranger, and instantly reach under his coat as though to snatch out a pistol or some weapon.

The man in brown scowled at the driver, shook his fist at him, and quickly disappeared behind the house opposite. The whole incident had only taken a minute, but Jared felt convinced that the heavy-browed rascal threatened some danger to the lady in the chaise.

"This red brick house is Mr. Nathaniel Carroll's," Norroy was saying. "The nearer door leads into the office where he transacts business."

"Thank you, sir," said the young woman. "Sebastien, drive up to the door."

Norroy walked down Prune Street, and Jared got up from his chair. He wondered who the visitor was and what evil the man in brown intended to the lady.

II

THE NECKLACE OF PEARLS

JARED pulled down his buff waistcoat and fingered his white stock and bow to make sure they were trim and in place. He was a sturdy fellow, of a dark complexion, with black eyebrows and hair. His coat and breeches were of brown broadcloth, well cut and new, though by no means so elegant as those of Henry Norroy.

There was a rap at the knocker, and he opened the outer door. On the step stood the lady of the chaise. " Is Mr. Nathaniel Carroll at home? " she asked, raising her blue eyes to Jared's.

"I think he is, madame. Will you be so good as to come in?" And with his best bow Jared stood aside to permit the lady to enter.

This she did, with a light step and a smile.

She was not tall—she hardly came up to Jared's shoulder—and of a slim, lithe figure. Her gown, of yellow cambric, sprigged with small flowers, was high waisted and long sleeved, and about her throat she wore a kerchief of the same color, the points tucked into her dress. Her blue silk hat, with its soft, puffed crown, was modish and very becoming.

Jared placed a chair for her, and she sat down.

"Mr. Carroll is probably still at dinner," he explained. "If you could wait a short time——"

"Most certainly," she said, with a trace of a foreign accent.

Jared took up a position opposite her, his hands clasped behind his back, an attitude copied from Mr. Carroll. "I saw your chaise through the window," he remarked. "Have you driven far?"

"From the Green Anchor Inn on the Delaware River." She added, "This is my first visit to Philadelphia."

"But not your last, I hope. The city is considered very attractive. Travellers declare it the finest this side of the Atlantic."

She smiled. "As to that I cannot judge, sir. I arrived in your country less than a month ago."

"Ah!" said Jared. "From Europe, of course?"

"From France. Oh, that poor country! It is like a den of wolves!"

Jared nodded. He had heard of the wild events of the French Revolution. "Yes," he agreed; "so all the letters say."

"No words can give a true picture of the situation," she hurried on. "Our unfortunate king and queen——"

A heavy step was heard in the hall that led from the house to the office. The young woman broke off and turned as the door opened and Nathaniel Carroll came in.

The lawyer glanced quizzically from the young woman, who sat perched on the edge of her chair, to Jared, who stood in front of her. Then Mr. Carroll bowed, and, shutting the hall door, came forward. He was a heavy man, tall and square-shouldered, and wore his hair powdered, though that custom was beginning to be abandoned by gentlemen of fashion.

"Your servant, madame," said Mr. Carroll. "I trust that, in my absence, Master Lee has seen to your entertainment." And his keen eyes, a little sly, glanced in his student's direction.

"He has been very kind," said the lady. "Are you, sir, Mr. Nathaniel Carroll?"

"That is my name. Whom have I the honor of addressing?"

"I am Mademoiselle Jeanne de Severac. I was sent to you by Mr. Simeon Oakes, who keeps the Green Anchor Inn. He said you would advise me."

Mr. Carroll again made a bow, then seated himself at his writing-table. "Oakes is a client of mine. An excellent fellow. Would you prefer, Mademoiselle de Severac, to speak to me alone?"

"Oh, not at all," she said with a slight flush.

Jared promptly sat down in his own chair. This, he thought, was likely to prove much more interesting than most of his preceptor's interviews with clients.

Mr. Carroll rubbed his hands together; he had had an excellent dinner. "Master Lee will attend us then. Your name, Mademoiselle de Severac, bespeaks a French origin."

"I am French, sir. My father is the Marquis de Severac, and until a short time ago he and I lived comfortably at our château in Normandy. What was going on in Paris and in other parts of the country had not touched our quiet village. We had heard reports, of course; but we believed that the government would soon set things to rights."

"No government is stronger than the people who compose it," observed Mr. Carroll. "I have no doubt, however, that ultimately law and order will supervene in France."

"But meantime, sir," said Mademoiselle Jeanne distressfully, "the Jacobins are destroying everything. They burned our château, and it was only by a miracle that my father and I escaped. We had thought that all the people were friendly to us— my father has always been kind to them—but they came one night, led by a man named Jacques Latour; they came armed, and they beat down our door.... Oh, sir, I don't know what they might not have done with us if we had not been able to fly before they found us! With one servant, Sebastien, we escaped to Havre."

"My poor young lady!" murmured Mr. Carroll. "The wretches! The *canaille!*"

"Indeed they were!" she assented. She hesitated, considering whether to narrate the incidents of their flight more in detail, then decided against it. "My mother was an Englishwoman; that is how I come to speak your tongue—and we have relations in that country, and thought that we would go there. But in Havre we found that all the ships to England were closely watched to see that none like us should escape to that country. That way was shut off. But Sebastien had a friend who brought us to the commander of an American ship, Captain Harvey, a kind man who offered to give us passage. And we came on his ship."

She sat back, her hands clasped in her lap, her face flushed and serious.

Jared, who had drunk in every word, was watching her with deeply sympathetic eyes.

"I should like to thank this Captain Harvey on behalf of my country," said Mr. Carroll. He cleared his throat and caught the lapels of his coat in his fingers. "To succor the unfortunate is the highest purpose of man. Permit me, mademoiselle, to offer you and your distinguished father, the Marquis, the hospitality of my home."

"Thank you, Mr. Carroll. My father is an elderly man, and much affected by all that has happened to us, or he would have come here today. Fortunately I am young and strong, and able to relieve him of some burdens. But I mustn't tire you with my story." She glanced at Jared, who gave her an encouraging smile. "Mr. Oakes, of the Green Anchor Inn, is a distant relation of Captain Harvey, and it was for that reason the Captain landed us there. He said that he would come back, but he had to sail to Norfolk, and now we hear there has been a terrible storm. We have had no news of him nor of his ship."

"There have recently been tremendous gales off the coast," stated Mr. Carroll. "However, let us hope Captain Harvey's ship outrode them."

"Without him," the French girl went on, "we have felt more friendless than ever. And we are in need of money, for we were able to bring very little gold with us. But fortunately I have some jewels. And so today I brought a necklace of pearls," she indicated a recticule that hung from her wrist; "I hoped you would be so kind as to direct me to a dealer who might buy it of me. Mr. Oakes said you knew everyone in Philadelphia."

Mr. Carroll bent his heavy brows, and made a peculiar sucking sound with his lips, a habit of his when he was reflecting. He prided himself on his ability to read people, and he found himself thoroughly believing this young woman's story. She was a gentlewoman; everything about her bespoke that. That she and her father, being aristocrats, had had to fly from their home in France, as she had described, was entirely credible. He did not like to think of her having to sell her pearls, but under the circumstances he could suggest no alternative. Doubtless the Marquis and his daughter would not care to accept a loan; and Mr. Carroll was averse to lending money on general principles.

"There is an honest goldsmith on High Street near Second," Mr. Carroll presently said; "Peter Parkinson by name. He does some business in precious stones. If you feel that you must sell the necklace—"

"Indeed, sir, I do."

"Then you could not do better than take it to him. Please mention my name. Mrs. Carroll sometimes deals with him."

The girl slipped from her chair. "A thousand thanks for your kind advice, Mr. Carroll. I—I have had no experience in business. Peter Parkinson, on High Street near Second."

Jared remembered the man he had seen spying on the girl and he said at once, "I will go with you."

Mr. Carroll cast a glance at his student, a twinkle

in his eye. "If Mademoiselle de Severac has no objection, that might be as well," he agreed.

"It would be very good of him," said the French girl, with a grateful smile that sent Jared instantly to the little cloak-room back of the office to get his hat.

"I trust," said Mr. Carroll, rising, "that your father, the Marquis, is going to give us the pleasure of his society—and yours—here in Philadelphia. Mrs. Carroll and I and our daughters would be delighted if he would. Aside from the pleasure of the personal acquaintance, it would be a great happiness to us to welcome guests from the country that sent us the gallant Lafayette. I had the honor of his acquaintance in those dark days when our land was going through the trials and tribulations that now beset France."

Mademoiselle Jeanne's blue eyes shone, and their charm was such that Mr. Carroll, his hand on his hip, was about to begin another peroration when Jared appeared, ready for the street. "Now, my boy," said Mr. Carroll, "see that Peter Parkinson deals honorably with this lady."

"Trust me, sir; I will," said Jared, bold as a lion.

Mr. Carroll ushered them out with a bow, and they walked to the waiting chaise, where Sebastien held the reins over a sleepy horse. Jared handed in the young woman and took the seat by her side.

Then, at his direction, Sebastien drove up Fourth Street to High, and down that to Second.

Meantime Jared, with many covert glances at his companion's piquant face, admirably set off by her big blue hat, supplied her with information concerning the sights they passed. Mademoiselle Jeanne, for her part, kept her eyes on the people, of whom there were many enjoying the fine spring day. And so, having made a pleasant, leisurely progress, they ultimately descended at the shop of Peter Parkinson.

The goldsmith, a little dried-up man, was within, and offered them chairs. Jared presented the lady, explaining that she was a friend of Mr. Nathaniel Carroll. Mademoiselle Jeanne took her necklace of pearls from her reticule and handed it to Parkinson, who carried it to the light at his front window and examined the pearls closely.

He came back, scratching his head. "I ask your pardon, madame, but would you be so good as to tell me something of the history of this chain?"

The French girl told him what she knew about it. The pearls had come to her from her mother.

"They are fine, but small," said the goldsmith. "In Europe there is much demand for ornaments of this nature, but not so much here in America. However, perhaps I might be able to offer you four hundred dollars for them. That is a considerable sum in our currency, as this gentleman knows."

"Four hundred dollars," repeated Jeanne, who had little enough idea of the purchasing power of these strange American coins.

"A large sum, isn't it, sir?" said Parkinson, looking at Jared. "Larger perhaps than I can afford; but considering that you are a friend of Mr. Carroll—"

"I think they're worth five hundred at the least," said Jared brazenly. "There are plenty of wealthy ladies in Philadelphia who would pay you more than that for them."

The goldsmith shook his head. "I don't know who the ladies are, sir. My profit at four hundred would be very small."

"Well," said Jared, "perhaps I can find a purchaser myself for them at five hundred. I'll interest Mrs. Carroll."

Parkinson scratched his cheek with a lean forefinger. "I'd like to oblige, so I would. But there's so much of chance in my business." He looked at the necklace again, and there was a shine in his deep-set eyes, something that Jared noted.

"Mademoiselle de Severac must have five hundred dollars," Jared declared firmly.

The goldsmith hesitated, and Jared reached out his hand for the necklace.

"Very well, very well," said Parkinson. "It's a very large sum, but I'll give it, considering you're a friend of Mrs. Carroll. If the lady will leave the

necklace with Mr. Carroll, I'll call for it in the
morning with the money."

Mademoiselle Jeanne appeared pleased with the
transaction. With a smile at the little man she took
the necklace from him and returned it to her reticule.
"I will speak to Mr. Carroll about it. If he will keep
it for me, that would be the better way. 'Tis a
long ride out the Chester Road to the Green
Anchor Inn."

"Aye, so it is, madame," nodded Parkinson. "And
it is not well to travel any of the roads south of
here at present with any amount of valuables or
money in one's possession. There's been more than
one report of robbery lately."

"Mr. Carroll will be glad to keep the pearls," asserted Jared. "Call tomorrow with the five hundred dollars in currency, Mr. Parkinson, and if Mr.
Carroll thinks the price a fair one, you shall have
the necklace."

With that he conducted the French girl to the
door, and again handed her to her seat in the chaise.
He felt very well pleased with himself; he had, he
considered, accomplished as much for Mademoiselle
Jeanne as any agent could have done.

Sebastien spoke to the sleepy horse and the chaise
turned westward. "I never thought there might be
a risk in bringing my necklace with me, Master Lee,"
said the girl. "I fear I have been very careless."

"We have it safe now," Jared responded lightly. "It's true there have been tales of highwaymen," he added, thinking, however, rather of the man in brown he had seen from the window than of thieves on the road.

"We must be home before nightfall. Sebastien is rather timorous about driving through a strange country."

It was then that Jared had an inspiration, but he said nothing about it at the moment.

Mr. Carroll was unengaged on their return, and listened to the story of their expedition. He looked at the pearls, and after some consideration—for he never liked to give an opinion too readily—he opined that he believed five hundred dollars was a satisfactory price. "And you have full authority from your father, mademoiselle, to dispose of them at any figure you think proper?" he asked Jeanne.

"They are my own property, sir. But my father gave me his approval of anything I might do with them."

"In that case, if you wish it, I will do as Parkinson suggests. I will keep the necklace in my strongbox until he delivers the money." Mr. Carroll turned to his writing-table, dipped a quill pen into an inkpot and drew several sheets of paper toward him. "I will draw up an authorization from you directing me to give him the necklace on receipt of the money,

and will hand you my receipt for the pearls.   When
we have the money we will send it to you at the
Green Anchor Inn."

The quill scratched over the paper for several
minutes, and the lawyer sprinkled the ink with sand
to dry it.   "Now, mademoiselle, will you be so kind
as to sign here?"

Jeanne took the pen and signed.   Mr. Carroll
himself signed the receipt and handed it to her.

She folded the paper and put it in her reticule,
then glanced at Jared.   "Thank you so much," she
said, "both of you gentlemen, for all your goodness
to me.   My father will feel himself immensely in
your debt."

Mr. Carroll waved his plump hand.   "My compli-
ments to your father on possessing such a daughter.
Mrs. Carroll is not at home this afternoon, or I
should give myself the pleasure of presenting you
to her.   But you must come to Philadelphia again.
Eh, Jared, Mademoiselle de Severac must come
here again?"

"I hope so," said Jared.   "And meantime, sir,
on account of the fact that her servant doesn't know
the country, and—er—on account of the fact that
there are stories about rough customers on the road,
I was intending to ride back with her to the
Green Anchor."

"Oh, no, you mustn't," said Mademoiselle Jeanne.

"I have a horse in the stable," he persisted, "and he needs exercise."

"I'm not in the least timorous," the girl protested.

Mr. Carroll's eyes twinkled. He was in truth, Jared's opinion to the contrary notwithstanding, a very human person. "There have been such stories," he agreed. "I think, mademoiselle, it might be as well for you to accept the escort of this young cavalier."

That settled it. Jeanne smiled. Jared, clapping on his hat, ran with long strides to the house where he lodged and got a pistol he had brought from the country. He saw that it was loaded, and then hastened to the neighboring stable where he kept his horse, and so expeditious was he that Mr. Carroll, standing at the curb of Fourth Street, was still in the middle of a speech to the girl in the chaise when Jared reappeared, astride his roan. The lawyer brought his eloquence to a close, and Sebastien flicked his mare.

They rode down Prune Street to Second and followed that to the ferry. Looking over his shoulder Jared caught sight of a man in brown jogging along on a horse some distance behind them. He did not see the man on the ferry as they crossed the Schuylkill River, but when they were on the other bank, riding south through the country, he saw the man again and felt sure he was following them. The stranger had some design on the French girl, and Jared was glad he had his pistol with him.

The chaise rolled south between orchards white and pink with apple and pear blossoms. Jared rode close at its side, chatting with Jeanne, alert and ready to protect her from any peril.

HE SAW THE MAN AGAIN AND FELT SURE HE WAS FOLLOWING THEM

III

THE HOSPITALITY OF JOSHUA MELLISH

TWILIGHT had settled on road and fields when the chaise and the horseman drew rein at the Green Anchor Inn. A cry of "Ho, hostler!" from Jared brought a boy running from the stables behind the tavern; Jared surrendered the roan to him and helped Mademoiselle Jeanne to alight.

The inn was rough-cast and of two stories. The little space between the front door and the road was filled with bleached oyster shells, which gave the appearance of a sea-beach. Not more than a stone's throw on the opposite side of the road flowed the broad Delaware, for the Green Anchor catered to guests from the river, masters and mates of ships bound up to Philadelphia or out to the ocean, making repairs or awaiting orders or finding any sort of plausible excuse for enjoying the hospitality of the shore.

"You'll not be riding back at once?" said Jeanne. "You'll stay to supper with my father and me?"

"It will give me great pleasure," said Jared.

They went up to the door, over which a massive hood projected, and into a wide hall. From this a room opened and therein were to be seen two gentle-men conversing at an oaken table.

"There is my father now," said Jeanne, and walked into the room.

One of the men looked up and rose, immediately followed by the other.

"Father, this is Master Lee," said the girl. "He is a student in Mr. Carroll's office in Philadelphia, and he has been so kind as to escort me back."

The gentleman addressed—a very thin figure in black, with fine eyes and an aquiline nose—bowed to Jared. "That was good of you, Master Lee. I am greatly indebted to you." He turned to the man who stood near him at the table. "Mr. Mellish, this is my daughter Jeanne. And the gentleman is, as you have heard, Master Lee of Philadelphia."

Mr. Mellish had a round, pleasant face and his plump body was buttoned into a tight green coat above a fawn-colored waistcoat. He bent to the hips as he was presented to the lady and he greeted Jared with an engaging smile. "I am honored, Mademoiselle de Severac. Master Lee, I am ac-quainted with the distinguished Nathaniel Carroll, a gentleman whose knowledge of the law is the admiration of all his fellow-citizens."

"Master Lee will stay to supper with us," said Jeanne, looking at her father.

"Master Lee will give me the pleasure of his company to supper at my house," Mellish corrected politely. "Your father, mademoiselle, has already accepted my invitation for you and himself."

The Marquis nodded. Mellish offered Jeanne a chair. "It was my good fortune," Mellish said in his pleasant, full voice, "to hear through my steward, who comes to the inn on occasion, that the Marquis de Severac and his daughter were staying here. Immediately I hoped that I might persuade the Marquis to become my guest. Therefore I drove over and presented myself to him. He has told me your situation—the distressing circumstances of your leaving your home in France—and his recital has increased a hundredfold my desire to show you hospitality. My house is not far from here, and it is at your disposal for as long as you care to remain."

"You are most generous, Mr. Mellish." Jeanne glanced at her father, and Jared saw that whatever her parent determined was law for her.

The Marquis had reseated himself. "Mr. Mellish is very generous, as you say, my dear. He has put his invitation in such a fashion—that of an American gentleman to two refugees from France—that I am glad to accept. Were conditions reversed— were he to be blown by evil winds to Normandy— I should wish to offer him shelter. I have told him our circumstances, the reason for your errand in

Philadelphia. And that reminds me, Jeanne, was your mission successful?"

"I am to get five hundred dollars for the pearls. Master Lee arranged that, and Mr. Carroll is to deliver the necklace to the purchaser tomorrow on receipt of the money."

The Marquis smiled sadly. "It is a new experience for one of us to have to sell our heirlooms."

Mellish thumped his hand on the table. "And this will be your last experience of such a kind, I hope!" he declared. "To think that the bearer of such an historic title as that of Marquis de Severac should find himself in such a predicament in America! The thought is insupportable! I am a republican, but I know what is due to the old nobility of France!"

His tone, rich and warm, his forceful attitude, his slightly empurpled face, thrilled and enthused Jared. "I agree with you, sir," he said heartily. "I am of your thought myself."

"Thank you, Master Lee," said Mellish. "Let us talk no more of selling heirlooms! It is settled then. You are to be my guests."

Thereupon he gave a great pull at the bell-rope that hung against the wall, so strong a pull that Simeon Oakes himself appeared in the doorway to see what was wanted.

"Oakes," said Mellish, "the Marquis and his daughter are going to take up their residence under my roof. Have a chaise ready for them, and send your boy upstairs to fetch their baggage."

"I shall want a few minutes in my room," said Jeanne. "I'll see to your packing, father."

"And now, Oakes," Mellish went on, when the girl had left the room, "three glasses of your best sherry before we take our departure."

The innkeeper was shortly back with the wine and the glasses. It being now dusk, he set a lighted candle on the table. Mellish raised his glass and bowed to the Marquis and Jared. "I drink to the ancient nobility of France," he said, "which has never shown itself more glorious than in the day of trouble."

Jared drained his glass. Already he felt a decided liking for this cheery man, who, although possibly a little more loud-spoken and less dignified than Mr. Carroll and his intimates, was clearly well-intentioned.

"And I," said the Marquis, "drink to my new acquaintances in this country across the sea. Really, gentlemen, your friendship has touched me deeply. I shall come to believe that all Americans are like the good Samaritan."

Mellish beamed, and wiped his lips with a large handkerchief. "And now, Marquis, if you will send Oakes for your hat and cloak, we might await your daughter at the chaise."

A young moon hung in the sky as the party left the Green Anchor. The de Severac baggage—which was small, for they had been able to bring little with them from France—was placed in the carriage. Sebastien drove the Marquis and his daughter, and Mellish and Jared rode their horses on either hand.

Half a mile away, and on a slope overlooking the river was the house of Joshua Mellish, a pretentious country structure, timbered and filled in with small bricks. A drive wound up to the front door, which was now lighted by a hanging lamp. At the sound of wheels a man-servant appeared and took his master's orders. The host led his guests into the hall, and summoned his housekeeper.

Bellevue was the name of the mansion, and it was a most capacious dwelling. Mellish was evidently a man of means and given to entertaining. His housekeeper heard his directions and conducted the Marquis and Jeanne to their apartments on the second floor. Jared was given in charge of a footman, who took him to a room where he might wash off the dust of travel.

Refreshed, Jared strolled into the drawing-room. A small fire burned on the hearth, and before it stood a young man, warming the backs of his legs. He had a thin, sharp-featured face and a long nose. His dress was irreproachable. His coat and breeches, of a light shade of mauve, his waistcoat, of white corded silk with a small embroidered figure and a border of flowers, were those of a dandy. With a wave of his hand he acknowledged Jared's presence.

"Welcome to Bellevue, sir," he said, "the haunt of beauty and of fashion. If I'm not mistaken, this would be your first visit to Joshua's lordly demesne."

"It is," Jared agreed. "I come from Philadelphia. My name is Lee."

"And mine is Skipworth, Cornelius Skipworth; at your service, Mr. Lee."

Jared crossed to the fireplace, noticing now that Mr. Skipworth's left eyelid drooped, thereby giving his face a satiric and somewhat owl-like expression. "Mr. Mellish is exceedingly hospitable," said Jared. "He was good enough to include me in his invitation to supper."

He was aware that the man in mauve was eyeing him from hair to shoe buckles, and that as he did so he was smiling to himself in a supercilious manner. "Hospitable? Oh, yes, there is no question as to that," said Skipworth. "Who are the other guests we are to have this evening?"

"The Marquis de Severac and his daughter, Mademoiselle Jeanne."

"A Marquis!" Skipworth thrust his thumbs into his waistcoat pockets and his smile broadened. "How the good Joshua does enjoy a title! This will inflate him still further, like a balloon. On my word, Mr.

Lee, you could have made no better entrance to Bellevue than in the train of a Marquis!"

Jared found the remark not to his liking. The pleasantry—if such it could be called—seemed to belittle both the host and his guests. "My own entrance—as you put it," he answered, "is entirely due to the fact that I rode to the Green Anchor Inn with Mademoiselle de Severac and that she asked me to sup with her father and herself before I returned to town."

"I meant no offence, my dear fellow. The situation simply amused me. I love Joshua like a brother —or perhaps I should say like a son—but affection should not blind us to the little peculiarities of those we may be fond of. What a dull world it would be if we lacked a sense of humor. 'Tis well worth the cultivating, Mr. Lee. Here comes Joshua now."

Mellish came in, rubbing his hands. His rosy face, his stout figure, even the gilt buttons on his coat seemed to radiate satisfaction. "Ah, Cornelius, you've introduced yourself to Mr. Lee? That's right. You two young blades ought to know each other. Mr. Lee is associated with Nathaniel Carroll in the practice of law; he could have no higher recommendation. Make friends with him, Cornelius, so that the next time you get into difficulties you'll know where to go for advice."

"We have a French lady and gentleman to supper, I understand," said Skipworth.

"The Marquis de Severac and his daughter," beamed the host. "They're to be my guests for a time. I count on you, Cornelius, to help in their entertainment."

"It will be a privilege; but I fear my French is somewhat rusty."

"They both speak beautiful English," said Mellish. "The French aristocracy, if I may judge from those I have had the honor of meeting, are the most cultivated people in the world."

"You should know." From his inflection, from his eye and smile Jared read the satirical nature that was hidden behind Skipworth's polished exterior. He did not like the man, although he admitted to himself that the fellow had a certain fascination.

At this point there were steps in the hall, and Jeanne and her father entered, the girl on the old man's arm.

Jeanne wore the same gown, but her hair was now uncovered and soft about her face. In the candlelight she seemed another person than the one he had ridden beside through the country that afternoon, more stately and more distant, but no less lovely or less full of grace.

Skipworth was presented, and Mellish, with Jeanne, led the way to supper.

At the table the French girl sat on the host's right hand, with Skipworth on her other side. The Marquis was opposite Mellish and Jared opposite Jeanne.

Mellish lived like a lord; one would have guessed from looking at him that he loved good fare. His napery, china, silver and glass were all of the most costly. Around a centrepiece of plaster of Paris depicting nymphs at play were grouped dishes containing venison, duck, and ham, parsnips, peas, and celery, rice-patties, jellies, cherry-tarts, oranges, nuts, figs and raisins. There was Madeira and Burgundy and a sweet, fragrant punch.

The talk was entertaining, and as Jared listened and observed he could not but admit to himself that there was a certain truth in what Skipworth had suggested, Mr. Mellish did take great delight in the company of people who belonged to what he constantly referred to as "the old nobility." Jared, however, saw no reason to criticize his host for that, he knew several very pleasant people in Philadelphia who were in the habit of mentioning their intimate acquaintance with personages of importance, and, though they sometimes amused him, he had never held it against them. Here at the supper table, however, this trait of Mr. Mellish's was continually brought to Jared's attention, and emphasized, by the sardonic smile of Skipworth, whose glance flickered across at Jared whenever their host grew unusually expansive.

Jared thought, moreover, that Jeanne did not altogether share her father's willingness to take Mr. Mellish at face value. Several times he caught a puzzled look on her face at something Mellish said. It seemed as if instinctively she felt a certain lack of breeding in him, something she was unaccustomed to among people of her own circle at home. Her father, for his part, was quite obviously satisfied with everything about his host. He listened with the utmost politeness and interest to all Mellish's stories, he complimented him on his wines, and when he could be induced to speak of his own recent experiences he did so with a reticence and a dignity that were superfine.

There was, it seemed to Jared, almost a child-like simplicity about the Marquis. And on the heels of this thought came the conclusion that it would be upon the shoulders of the daughter rather than on those of the father that would rest the responsibility of judging new acquaintances and determining the wisest course of action in their altered circumstances. It would be she who would protect her father.

As to Cornelius Skipworth, Jared could see that he was a man of many social lights and shades. To the Marquis he spoke as one gentleman to another, tinged with the deference that is due from youth to age; to Mellish his tone was that of a brusque raillery, he said things that were capable of two meanings; and to Mademoiselle Jeanne his speech and his whole bearing were those of a courtier to a queen. Jared alone he seemed at times to take into his confidence, when his hooded eye lifted and his glance met that of the younger fellow, whom he regarded with the half-mocking patronage of the older schoolboy for the lad just entered at school.

They rose and went into the drawing-room, and now Jared felt that he must take his departure. He said so to Mellish, who clapped him on the shoulder, and invited him to come to Bellevue again. Jared spoke to the Marquis, who thanked him for escorting his daughter from town and expressed the hope of a further acquaintance with him. Then the young man turned to the girl, who was at the moment chatting with Skipworth near the door into the hall.

"I must say good-night, mademoiselle."

"You have been very kind, Master Lee."

Skipworth glided away, and Jared felt more at ease.

"I hope that when Mr. Carroll receives your money from Parkinson he will let me bring it to you."

Her blue eyes shifted under his steady gaze. "That

would be very considerate of you. Perhaps then
this is only *au revoir*, Master Lee—depending on
Mr. Carroll." She extended her hand.

Jared lifted it to his lips. *"Au revoir,* mademoiselle, whether Mr. Carroll sends me or no."

She nodded, smiled, made him a curtsy, and so
dismissed him.

In the hall a servant handed him his hat and
said that his horse was ready. Jared went out into
the cool spring night, now bathed in starlit beauty.

Someone was strolling on the lawn, and as the
groom surrendered the roan to its master, Skipworth
stepped up. "You'll be coming to Bellevue again,
of course, Mr. Lee," he said. "Everyone does.
Joshua likes you, and I'll not say it's due entirely
to Nathaniel Carroll nor the Marquis; no, it's on
account of your own *beaux yeux,* as the French say.
The new guests are charming. Naturally, however,
they brought little gold from France."

"Naturally they couldn't, leaving in haste," said
Jared.

"Maybe it's as well they haven't much gold,"
mused Skipworth. He paused a moment. "This is
one of Bellevue's quiet evenings. The next time
you come you'll find us more gay. You like pleasure, I suppose?"

"Of course I do," Jared laughed.

"With a dash of recklessness in it? Well, remember, my boy, that the country isn't as sober—or as safe, for that matter—as Philadelphia. Be off with you, Master Lee, I'll see that no harm comes to your French friends."

Jared, somewhat puzzled by Skipworth's words, somewhat annoyed by his superior manner, mounted his horse and rode down the drive. What harm could come to his French friends in the country? He was still wondering about this when, as he reached the end of the woods and was about to turn into the highroad, a man stepped out of the bushes in front of him. Jared pulled up the roan and instantly laid hand on his pistol.

"Where are the Frenchman and his daughter?" came the question in a deep, throaty voice from the man in the road.

"That's none of your business," answered Jared.

"It is my business," said the other. "You don't know who they are. They're traitors to their country; they've run away from France."

"Get out of my way!" ordered Jared.

"I warn you to have nothing to do with them."

"And I warn you to stand away from my horse."

The man muttered something. "You're trying to protect them. You rode out with her from the city. I'll teach you—"

Instantly Jared was at him, and as the man reached for his bridle Jared struck him over the head with the butt of his revolver. The fellow reeled away, and Jared clapped heels to his horse. With a bound they were in the highroad.

For a moment he hesitated—should he go back and tell the Marquis about the man in brown who had dogged Jeanne's footsteps all day? Then he remembered that their servant, Sebastien, had also seen and recognized the rascal and would doubtless tell his master of him if he thought it needful. There was nothing to be gained by his rousing Jeanne's fears; and what could happen to her or to her father while they were under the protection of such a host as Joshua Mellish?

He rode on, excited by his adventure. The man in brown was behind him, well out of his way, but he kept a sharp lookout, for this was the section of country, so the rumors said, frequented by the highwayman.

IV

JARED MEETS TWO FARMERS

THE night was fine and clear, the footing good, and Jared didn't pull up until he came to a place where two roads intersected. Here on his left was a low, rambling farmhouse, now entirely dark. After a little consideration he decided that the road he wanted was the one to the right.

On this he had not gone more than a hundred yards when he heard voices in front of him and slowed up his horse. The voices appeared to be those of two men quarrelling. Cautiously—for he didn't know what stratagems highwaymen might use to lure on their victims—he gripped his pistol with his fingers. A few more yards and he was close behind the two who were talking so loudly. They were mounted and between them filled up the width of the road. He must either stop or push past them, and deciding on the more valiant course, Jared called out, "Hola there! Let me by, will you?"

The two in front of him turned, and Jared eyed them narrowly, his pistol on his saddle-bow. One was a big stout man in a beaver hat and long cloak, the other, a much smaller fellow, wore a three-cornered hat and close-fitting jacket. They stared at

Jared, but did not immediately make way for him, and so he was forced to edge his roan along at the side of the highway.

"Did you pass a man on a black horse, a villain with a patch over one eye?" asked the stout man, twisting round in his saddle.

"With a cloak up to his ears and a hat drawn down to his nose?" added the small one.

Jared shook his head.

"We've been robbed," announced the stout one. "A hundred dollars between us."

"We were riding along the other road, the one from Chadd's Ford," said his companion, "when a man rode out from a clump of trees and held us up at the point of a pistol. A tall man on a black horse."

"A smooth villain," said the first man; "an old hand at such business, I'll swear!"

"If I'd been behind, as you were, Thomas," said the other, "I wouldn't have put my hands up so quick."

"If I'd been you, I wouldn't have done his bidding so quick, Samuel," retorted the stout rider. "You could have given me a chance to get my pistol out."

"Get your pistol out! You had your hands up, and sat there shaking like a jelly!"

"You could have ducked down behind my horse and opened my saddle-bag."

"With him right atop of me, you fool!"

They were glaring at each other and shaking their fists, as they had been doing when Jared first saw them.

It was not a laughing matter, and yet Jared could not help smiling. Each of them was so busy blaming the other after the event.

"There have been reports in Philadelphia of highwaymen on this road," Jared observed, for he was now convinced they were innocent travellers.

"Oh, we'd heard the reports," said the small man. "That's why we were armed. But my brother would carry his pistol in his saddle-bag."

"You rode in front!" snorted Thomas. "And you had your pistol in your belt!"

"Where a man ought to carry it, if he isn't a great lumbering cheese! I couldn't get my pistol out," the small man explained to Jared, "because before I knew what was happening the villain was on top of me, ordering me to put up my hands."

"What did he do?" asked Jared, wondering that two armed men should allow themselves to be trapped so easily by a single horseman.

"He had his pistol aimed at my head," stated Samuel, "and he rode up close to me and jerked my pistol from my belt. Then he made me dismount and fetch him Thomas's saddle-bags. When I'd done that he helped himself to my bags, and coolly rode off, wishing us a pleasant journey. Thomas's

4

pistol was in his bag and so was half the money, in coin; and the other half was in my bag."

"He must have known something about you," said Jared; "that is, about the money you carried."

"Samuel talks about his business to everyone," declared Brother Thomas. "I expect every man, woman and child in Chadd's Ford knew we were taking currency to Mr. Norris's counting-house in Philadelphia."

"There you go! Talking to a stranger! It's you who are the great talker!"

"Well," Jared interposed, seeing that they were about to turn on each other again, "the milk's spilled this time. I daresay the man with the patch over his eye is ten miles away by now."

"I shall see the authorities in Philadelphia about this," said Thomas. "The villain ought to be hanged."

"You'll make yourself ridiculous," said Samuel. "Sitting there, with your hands up, behind me, and your pistol in your saddle-bag!"

"We should have planned to be in the city before nightfall," stout Brother Thomas asserted.

"And whose fault is it that we weren't?" Brother Samuel retorted. "We would have been there before sundown if you hadn't stopped at every public-house along the road for a bite and a drink."

Jared thought he had never seen such an absurd

pair as these brothers, and, having no desire to listen to their further quarrels, he spoke softly to his roan and rode on. He had not gone more than twenty yards, however, when the big, cloaked rider trotted up alongside. "He'll talk me deaf and dumb," he said. "I won't hearken to any more of his twaddle. 'Tis bad enough to be robbed, without being belabored with hard words into the bargain."

Jared smiled, but said nothing, and they rode along together for some minutes in silence, the other brother keeping to himself in the rear.

"A pistol is a most uncomfortable object to wear in one's belt," said Jared's companion. "It grinds into my side. That was the reason I carried it in my saddle-bag."

"I can quite understand," agreed Jared, determined that he, at least, should not be drawn into any argument.

"You talk like a sensible fellow. The whole affair happened so quickly I had no time to collect my wits. If I had had a moment or two to consider the situation I assure you the villain wouldn't have come off so easy."

"Doubtless," agreed Jared.

They rode on in silence. Behind them, at some distance, came the rat-a-tat of the other horseman. Once Jared looked over his shoulder and caught a

glimpse of Brother Samuel, a small, morose figure
in the starlight.

The highway now ran nearer to the river and
sleeping farmhouses began to increase in number.
"You are from Philadelphia?" asked Jared's companion.

"Yes. You're familiar with the city?"

"Entirely so. My home is at Chadd's Ford, but
I come to town frequently. I usually put up at the
City Tavern in Second Street. I like their veni-
son pie."

"So do I," grinned Jared.

"And their beefsteak cooked with onions," continued the other. " Yes, every so often I feel the
need of coming to the city for business and refreshment." He gave a sigh. "To be robbed of a hundred dollars is hard, but fortunately my credit is
good with the landlord."

They came to the lower ferry, and, now joined
by the other brother, crossed to the town. Up
Second Street they trotted, with frequent glimpses
of the shining river through lanes and alleys on
their right.

Near the corner of Walnut they reined in, before a wide, lighted building. "Here I stop," said
Brother Thomas. "Good-evening to you, sir." With
a bob of the head he turned his horse in the direction
of the inn-yard.

Brother Samuel, on the other side of Jared, took off his three-cornered hat and scratched his head. "He'll forget all about our trouble over a glass of ale," he said sourly. "He ought to be counting the pennies, not treating himself to the best. However, I'll not have him eating and drinking here, and me going supperless to bed. Good-night, sir." And he also rode off to the inn-yard.

A pretty pair! thought Jared. The man who had held them up must have found them easy picking! There was about as much fight in either of them as in a feather bed. But their enforced society left him with a desire for something more palatable, and so, sliding down from his roan, he tied the horse to a sapling at the curb and went into the tavern.

The main room was large and furnished with many tables. Most of these were now unoccupied, for the hour was fairly late. In one corner, however, a group of young men were gathered, talking volubly and dipping their noses into big tankards of ale.

Jared advanced to this table, and was loudly hailed. "Welcome, Master Jared! Welcome to our circle!"

"Behold Demosthenes, the silver-tongued!"

"Waiter, a foaming flagon for the learned judge!"

"Draw up, Jared, and tell us the news. What kept you so long this evening?"

The new-comer, his hands on the back of a chair

that had been pushed toward him, said, "I have news of a highwayman."

"The deuce you have!" exclaimed Henry Warder. "Is he promenading Second Street?"

"Did you see him?" asked Michael Cornish.

"I met two horsemen on the Chester Road; they were coming from Chadd's Ford," said Jared, "and they'd been held up by a highwayman and eased of their saddle-bags, which contained a hundred dollars in coin."

The waiter brought a tankard of ale, and Jared sat down and washed the dust of the road from his throat. To his audience he told his story, not omitting any detail of the conduct of the two brothers, and indeed drawing considerably on his imagination when he described what must have been the appearance of the two with their hands above their heads.

"Dash me, if I don't think the robber more deserving of the money than two such timid loons!" exclaimed Timothy Inglis, a red-haired fellow in a coat of blue. "And he'll doubtless know how to spend it better than any pursy, fat farmer. I wish the highwayman luck!" He drank from his tankard, and rapped on the table for the waiter to bring him a fresh one.

"Shame on you, Timothy!" drawled Michael Cornish. "Don't you know that the law must be respected, and that Jared is studying diligently how to respect it?"

A short fellow, who sat hunched up in his chair, his arms crossed on the table, here observed, "We haven't heard what Jared was doing on the Chester Road, out in the wild, uncivilized country."

"That's so," said Warder. "It seems that an explanation is required of such unusual conduct."

"I'd been to the Green Anchor Inn," said Jared, "on business connected with Mr. Carroll's office."

"A circumspect answer," said Cornish. "Note with what skill the legal mind draws a veil over all the important points of a case. For instance, it is to be presumed that Jared had supper at the inn, that he had company at supper—"

"Not so loud, Michael," interrupted Warder. "Here come some strangers. Don't give Jared away."

Heads were turned as two men came into the room and seated themselves at a table at the opposite end. A waiter immediately went up to them.

"The two I was telling you of," whispered Jared to his friends. "The affectionate brothers."

"They look to me," said Inglis, "as if they'd bite each other's head off for a shilling."

"Don't pay any attention to them," begged Jared, "or the fat one will be over here. He has a decided liking for my society."

"What were we discussing?" began Warder. "Oh, yes, Jared's business at the Green Anchor. That inn is, I believe, chiefly frequented by sea-faring men."

"A very questionable place," put in Cornish, "for a young gentleman of good reputation. Sea-faring men are notoriously an evil lot. It surprises me that Mr. Carroll should have allowed his student to run the risk of such contamination."

"Waiter," called Jared, "fetch Mr. Cornish more ale. He's talking himself dry."

"Hello, here's Norroy," said Warder, who sat in view of the front door.

The circle turned and a babel of voices rose in vociferous greeting. With a wave of his hand, as if to still the tumult, the tall, fresh-colored man in the plum coat and light yellow breeches walked up to the group.

"Sit down, Hal!" "Better late than never!" "Another tankard, waiter, a large one for Mr. Norroy."

"I see the club is largely attended tonight," smiled Norroy. "Are we debating matters of pith and moment?"

"That we are," said Cornish. "Jared here had a narrow escape from being held up by a highwayman on the Chester Road."

"You needn't shout so everyone can hear," protested Jared, and added to Norroy, who had taken a chair beside him, "Those are the victims over there. I've had enough of them for one night."

Norroy glanced over his shoulder. "It hasn't taken away their appetites," he commented. "Tell me the story."

Jared outlined his adventure, while Norroy drank his ale.

At the conclusion Norroy nodded. "Well, now, my lad, you'll have something more to tell the worthy Nathaniel Carroll than mere tavern gossip. And speaking of Mr. Carroll—" He looked at the group, who, having heard Jared's recital before, had turned their attention to a story from Michael Cornish, then edged his chair away from the table, and lowered his voice. "Speaking of Mr. Carroll, how did you fare with the charming young lady who called this afternoon?"

"I was able to do her a little service," Jared answered, also withdrawing his chair so that he and Norroy sat somewhat removed from the others. "She is a French lady, the daughter of the Marquis de Severac. She is new to this country, and so, for her greater safety, I rode out with her to the Green Anchor Inn, where she and her father were staying."

"Gallant as ever! I envy you," sighed Norroy, though his eyes twinkled. "And that was how you came to be on the Chester Road when those two guzzling farmers met with their misadventure?"

"I stayed to supper. But not at the inn. A gentleman named Mellish, who lives nearby, had invited the Marquis and his daughter to be guests at his house, and he included me. He has a fine place, called Bellevue. Do you know him?"

"Do I know Joshua Mellish? That I do, Master Jared!" Norroy's eyes danced over the rim of his tankard.

"Do you know his friend, Cornelius Skipworth? He was there tonight."

"Aye, I know Skipworth. And so our blue-eyed lady has taken up her abode at Bellevue? Did I understand you rightly? The lady and her father are staying there?"

"For the present, yes. Who is Mr. Mellish? He seemed a very likeable man."

"Oh, he is; uncommonly likeable. There never was such a man for doing a favor for a friend. If the charming little lady and her father, the Marquis, have gained the friendship of Joshua Mellish I think we may consider their comfort assured. They will live on the choicest of viands and sleep in the softest of beds. But you saw his house and you had supper there; that ought to be sufficient to convince you of the truth of what I say."

"Yes," Jared agreed. "But you haven't told me much about the real man."

"A bachelor, rich, with a love of entertaining.

Were there other guests there this evening besides the French gentleman, his daughter, Skipworth, and yourself?"

Jared shook his head. "Skipworth told me it was one of Bellevue's quiet evenings. And he asked me if I liked pleasure with a dash of recklessness."

"And you said you did, of course." Norroy was silently laughing—that is, his eyes were—at his neighbor, who was so evidently interested in the subject they were discussing. "You must see Bellevue on one of its really festive evenings, when it becomes the shrine of the Goddess of Chance. Mellish has many guests there at such a time—you'd be surprised how many ladies and gentlemen of fashion in Philadelphia are eager to go to his parties. You shall go with me some evening; but—a whisper in your ear—I wouldn't mention it to Mr. Carroll or his good wife."

"Most certainly not. I'd like to go with you, Hal. It sounds exciting."

"And a student of law requires some excitement once in a while, eh?" Norroy's gaze became meditative. "Matters are looking up, my boy. You were downcast this afternoon, but this evening I warrant you're finding circumstances fairly supportable."

Thereupon Norroy pushed his chair closer to the table and joined in the talk of the group. What a fascinating personality he had, Jared reflected. Yes, it would be exciting to go with him to one of Mellish's parties.

Presently Jared rose. "You lads sleep to all hours in the morning," he said, "but I have to be up betimes."

"I, too," chimed in Norroy. "I'll go with you, Jared."

They paid their scores, said their good-nights, and turned to the tavern door. As he crossed the room Jared glanced at the two brothers at their table, and the stout one caught his eye and nodded to him.

Jared returned the bow and hurried out. After him came Norroy. "What a blessing it is to have a passion for anything, even for meat and drink," observed the latter. "Your friend of the heavy jowl has forgotten his mischance in a venison pastry."

"The great lout!" muttered Jared.

"Nay, you're too hard on people. Heaven forbid they should all be run in the same mould!"

"You're a philosopher, Hal."

"Aye, a bit of one, I'll admit," said Norroy with a smile.

They came out into the street, but before they parted Norroy laid his hand on Jared's arm. "There's a lesson for you, my boy, in the adventure of those two farmers. The streets of the city are safe, but beware how you ride the country roads after nightfall."

"I was armed," said Jared. "And watched every tree and shadow."

"That's right," nodded his friend.

"And Mr. Mellish's place is safe, isn't it?" asked Jared, thinking of the French pair.

"There are no highwaymen there, if that is what you mean," answered Norroy. "But there are good people in this town who would shun Bellevue like the plague. Pleasure with a dash of recklessness, as Skipworth described it—that suits it well." With a laugh and a slap on Jared's back Norroy turned and walked up Walnut Street.

Jared untied his horse, wondering if Jeanne and her father had done well or ill in accepting Mr. Mellish's invitation. He decided to keep an eye on them. There was the man in brown to be considered, and from what Norroy had said, Bellevue itself seemed to be a questionable harbor.

V

THE SHIP CHANDLER

THE sun had already risen some distance in the heavens when Jared stirred on his feather bed and opened his eyes. His window stood wide open and the white curtains were blowing inward on a gentle, springtime breeze. On the plank floor, scrubbed to whiteness, lay a shaft of yellow light that reached to the edge of the hooked rug in front of his lowboy. Luxuriously he stretched his arms, then crossed them under his head on the pillow. The events of the preceding afternoon and evening were trooping back to his mind and giving him food for thought.

In the midst of his reflections, however, there came a knock at his door and the slightly nasal voice of Mrs. Bird, saying, "It's time to be up, Master Lee." For the present he had to abandon the study of his gallery of new faces and personalities; the courtly, guileless French Marquis; his vivacious, blue-eyed daughter; the rubicund Joshua Mellish; the sardonic Skipworth with his hooded eye; the absurd brothers from Chadd's Ford, whom he had met on the road. With an answering "I'm up, Mrs. Bird!" he sprang out of bed and embarked on his toilet. The detail that occupied him the longest was the arranging of

62

his white stock and bow, for by the smartness of these
articles of apparel was a young man judged by
his world.

Descending to the dining-room, he found that his
landlady had breakfast ready, and he quickly disposed of his sliced ham and fried eggs, bread and
butter and cup of tea.   Then, delaying only to brush
his beaver hat, he left Mrs. Bird's house and walked
the three squares to Mr. Carroll's office with long
energetic strides.

As usual, his preceptor had not yet appeared from
his dwelling, and Jared busied himself with seeing
that the inkpots were filled, the quill pens ready
for use, and the books and papers properly arranged.
He was still thus engaged when through the hall door
Nathaniel Carroll entered, his younger daughter,
Hannah, hanging on his arm.

"Good-morning, sir," said Jared.   "Good-morning, Miss Hannah."

Mr. Carroll inclined his head.

"Good-morning, Master Jared," said Hannah,
releasing her father's arm.   She was a plump girl
of seventeen, rosy-cheeked and brown-eyed, but
much too unformed as yet in either face or figure
to be pretty in Jared's estimation.

"Father told us last evening of his caller, the
young French lady," Hannah continued.   "He said

you were going to ride with her all the way out to the Green Anchor Inn."

" 'Tis not such a very long ride," said Jared; "and my mare needed exercising." He spoke in the lofty manner of a man addressing a too inquisitive child.

Hannah wrinkled her nose and stuck out the tip of her tongue, two tricks which she had found by experience were distasteful to this superior law-student of her father's. And while Mr. Carroll proceeded to the arm-chair at his writing table, his daughter fixed her round brown eyes on Jared. "Father says she was very pretty in a big, puffed blue hat. And did you talk French to her?"

"The lady preferred to speak English," Jared responded in a haughty fashion. However, his knowledge of the French tongue induced him to add, "I could have used her language. I am fairly well familiar with it, having learned it from a Frenchman who came here during the war and stayed to work on my father's farm."

"Oh yes, I remember," said Hannah. "How nice that you can speak French! Father says the young lady's mother was English."

Jared glanced at Mr. Carroll, seeking an opportunity to change the conversation, but the lawyer was busy reading a letter he had taken from an envelope.

"Did she ask you to stay to supper?" Hannah went on.

"She did," said Jared, and added loftily, "I had the honor of being presented to her father."

"He's a Marquis, isn't he?"

"I believe he is."

"Is the French lady coming to Philadelphia again soon?"

"Really I don't know. She didn't mention her plans to me."

"Elizabeth and I think it would be nice if mother would invite her here," went on the undaunted Hannah. "Foreign people are always so interesting."

"Sometimes they are," said Jared, and, turning to his table, he opened a book.

"Didn't you find this one entertaining?"

"A lady who has suffered all the experiences that Mademoiselle de Severac has," Jared stated, "is bound to be interesting. Her views on present conditions in France are very enlightening."

"I suppose so. You learned a good deal from her, didn't you, Master Jared—about conditions in France?"

Mr. Carroll looked up from his letter. "Hannah, my dear, isn't it time you were busy with your housekeeping duties? I think I heard your mother say you were going to market with her."

"Yes, father." Hannah cast a glance at the broad

back of the young fellow who appeared to be reading his book. "I'm sure we'd all like to hear about the Marquis and his daughter from Master Jared when he isn't so busy with his law studies." With a flounce of her skirts she tripped out of the office, stopping at the door a moment to thrust the tip of her tongue at Jared, who had looked over his shoulder.

Jared after a moment walked over to the door and closed it. Discussion of business affairs ought not to be overheard by irresponsible young creatures like Hannah and Elizabeth Carroll.

"I gather from what you say that your escort of Mademoiselle de Severac was successful," Mr. Carroll remarked, leaning back in his chair.

"I think I may say so, sir. Her father asked me to convey to you his thanks for your assistance."

"They are comfortably lodged at the Green Anchor?"

"They have moved from the inn. A Mr. Joshua Mellish has invited them to stay with him."

Mr. Carroll's heavy brows went up in a look of surprise and he pursed his lips. "Mellish! Indeed!"

"I supped with them at Mr. Mellish's. I should think they would be very comfortable there."

"Well, let's hope they may be." The lawyer picked up a document and unfolded it. "I thought the young lady a person of refinement. Yes, exceedingly refined and—ah—unworldly. I trust that no unscrupulous person will take advantage of her father. There are, I regret to say, people who make it a business to prey on innocent foreigners."

"And not always on foreigners," said Jared. "You remember what I told you the other day about highwaymen? Last night, as I was riding home, I met two farmers from Chadd's Ford who'd been held up on the road, and robbed of a hundred dollars."

"Dear me! That's most unfortunate! Conditions in the country aren't what they should be. I never like to travel over country roads at night."

Mr. Carroll spread out the document on the table, picked up pen and paper, and began making notes. Jared subsided into his own chair, and fell to copying laboriously the terms of a deed.

Half an hour passed in silence except for the scratching of the quills. Then clients began to arrive and confer with Mr. Carroll. Presently Peter Parkinson appeared with a bag containing five hundred dollars. The money was carefully counted, Mademoiselle de Severac's pearl necklace produced from the strongbox, and the transfer duly made. The strongbox, with the money in it, was locked in a closet and Mr. Carroll pocketed the key.

At one o'clock Jared returned to Mrs. Bird's for dinner, and, having eaten hastily, allowed himself a period of recreation before going back to work.

Today, as frequently, his steps led him in the direction of the river, where were the most interesting sights for a fellow like himself, brought up in the country. He strolled along the wharves, past the warehouse of Stephen Girard, the great merchant, and stopped to admire the ships unloading or taking on cargoes. The breeze brought him a mixture of strange, penetrating odors that stirred his blood and made him think of distant, mysterious lands. And then he turned in at the door of a little shop wedged in between two tall buildings, the place of business of Simon Duckett, ship's chandler, a man whom Jared had come to know fairly intimately since first meeting him at Nathaniel Carroll's office early in the winter.

Duckett was eating bread and ham from the flat top of a cask in the rear of his shop. He was a small man, in shirt sleeves and a big leather apron, with bright eyes and a skin weathered and tanned. "Come in, Jared," he invited. "Have you had dinner. If you haven't—" He waved his knife at the loaf of bread and the dish of sliced ham.

"I have, thank you, Simon. I was passing by, and I just dropped in for a minute, to get a whiff of your tar and varnish before going back to my desk."

"It's dull mulling over those papers and books,

ain't it, lad? You'd rather be sailing the high seas, wouldn't you? the way I did when I was your age."

"I'd rather be doing a number of things. But what's the good of wishing? I've got to make my fortune; and you know the old saying, 'A rolling stone gathers no moss.'"

"I've known a number of rolling stones that gathered a good bit of moss," said Duckett, cutting a slice of bread and placing a layer of ham across it. "But most of them wasn't respectably brought up like you be."

Jared smiled and his eyes roved around the back part of the shop, which was so cluttered with boxes, bales, kegs, ironmongery, pieces of canvas, coils of rope, that it seemed a miracle the owner could ever find anything he wanted. On cold winter afternoons, when there was ice in the Delaware and the wind went screeching through the narrow lanes and alleys, this place, its doors shut, smelling of tar and oakum, was a haven where one might be snug and talk of storms and wrecks. Today, however, snugness was not so desirable, the look and odors of the shop made one think of white sails skimming over a shining sea, of the lift and heel of a deck, of cool green waters sliding past, of the salt breeze in one's nostrils. And Simon Duckett, sinewy, tanned, grizzled, in his leather apron seemed to belong to the ocean as much as any of the articles he dealt in. He had been one of the crew of the *Bon Homme Richard* when the great American Captain, Paul Jones, had fought and overcome the English frigate *Serapis*.

"Don't you ever feel," said Jared, "as if you'd like to step aboard one of these ships in the river and sail away in her?"

"Oh, yes, there's times when I do. But I've got a wife and a couple of youngsters to care for. A man can't have everything. He's got to decide what 'tis he wants the most, and stick by his bargain." Duckett finished munching his bread and ham and wiped his hands on his apron. "Don't you get it in your head, Jared, that a sailor's life is all beer and skittles. A man's safer ashore."

"Of course there are storms, and sometimes leaky vessels."

"Yes, and there's more than that. There's bad captains and mates and bad sailors. I've known captains who should have been hung at the yard-arm, and I've seen sailors strung up there, who well deserved what they got. And there's privateers, which is a nice way of saying pirates; the sea's full of them these days."

"You mean because of the war between England and France?"

"You can lay it to that, or to the natural devil-try there is in men. Letters-of-marque! It don't need letters-of-marque or any other kind of excuse for a natural born buccaneer to lay hands on a rich cargo. The sea's wide, and it's easy enough for him to say he's French or English or anything else, as best suits his purpose, if he's overhauled and questioned. Aye, Jared, when a ship sails nowadays, right here out o' the Delaware, there's no knowing where she'll fetch up. There's been more than one this past year that's never been heard of again."

"I thought they were English or French ships, captured by privateers."

"Aye, that's what many think. But if they spent their time on the wharves as I do they'd know different. Anything can happen at sea. You don't know how easy it is for a ship to disappear and nobody but her crew and the men who wrecked her be any the wiser. Privateers?" Duckett chuckled. "I call them pirates, same as was Blackbeard. They lie off the Capes, flying a foreign flag; they signal a pilot boat and capture her. Then the crew go aboard and when an inbound vessel signals for assistance in entering the river, the pirates answer the signal and plunder her. Plenty of excuses, of course; orders of their government and so forth. I ain't saying the French and English are shining saints; but there's a lot that goes on off the Delaware Capes that don't rightly belong on their shoulders."

"I should think," said Jared, "there would be some

way to stop such plundering. Our new national government—"

"Our new government," Duckett interrupted, "is trying to do a thousand things at once, without the proper men or implements, or enough money, to do a half of them. Can men like General Washington or Alexander Hamilton or our own Robert Morris give their time and thought to the loss of a few cargoes off the coast? 'Tis the business of the merchants and ship owners, and they're so jealous of each other they won't raise a finger for their common good." He wrapped the half loaf of bread in a piece of paper and put it in a cupboard. "I'm telling you this so you won't run away to sea, as I did. A sailor's lot isn't all fun; it never has been and never will be."

"I wasn't thinking of doing anything of the kind, Simon," laughed Jared.

"No, and don't you get to thinking of it," said the chandler. "You're a deal better off in Mr. Carroll's office, reading law and talking to rich clients."

Jared bent his steps back to the brick house at the corner of Fourth and Prune Streets. According to his custom at this hour, Mr. Carroll was partaking of a lengthy dinner with his family. Jared sat down at his table, opened a book, and began to read. But he couldn't keep his mind on the context, and after half-a-dozen herculean efforts he slid down in his seat until his head rested against the back of the chair, shut his eyes, and dozed.

He woke with a start. Mr. Carroll's heavy step was in the hall. Hastily leaning forward, the student's eyes were glued to the page of his book when the lawyer came into the room.

Mr. Carroll nodded. "Your diligence does you credit, Jared," said he. "A thorough knowledge of the fundamentals of jurisprudence is an essential to success at the bar. Let Blackstone's Commentaries be your Bible on weekdays. *Magna est vis consuetudinis,* which, being translated, means great is the force of habit. When the mind is trained so that one thinks naturally in the terms of law, the problems that are presented to one for elucidation resolve themselves easily. I myself have found it so." Mr. Carroll, as usual, had enjoyed his dinner, and was now agreeably expansive.

Jared listened politely while the lawyer, pacing the floor of the office with dignified tread, delivered his homily. At its conclusion Mr. Carroll stopped, adjusted his waistcoat and smoothed his coat. "To come down to the business of the day," he said, "there was something I meant to tell you. What was it? What was it?" He tapped his forehead with his finger. "Oh, yes, I remember now. I sent Parkinson's five hundred dollars out to Mademoiselle de Severac by special messenger, by Jacob

Gilroy, a trusty man whom I frequently employ on such missions. I told Gilroy he would find the lady at the house of Mr. Mellish."

Mr. Carroll wasn't looking at Jared as he spoke— he was gazing at a row of substantial volumes on the opposite wall—but if he had been looking he would have seen a flush rise in the young man's face.

"I thought you had it in mind, sir, to let me do that errand. I'm familiar with the road."

"So is Gilroy. As I've said, I often employ him."

Jared turned in his chair. He felt hotly indignant. Mr. Carroll had known that he wanted to complete the business he had begun. But there was no use in words, Gilroy was already on his way to Bellevue, Jared couldn't overtake him now, even if Mr. Carroll might be persuaded to let him try it.

What would Mademoiselle Jeanne think of him, allowing a hired messenger to do a service he had told her he hoped to do himself?

He glanced at Mr. Carroll, who was now taking a bundle of papers from a secretary on the other side of the room. What a stiff-necked man the lawyer was!

"We must always remember that in business matters business methods are the best," remarked Mr. Carroll. "Gilroy will deliver the money to the lady at Mellish's house and take a receipt for it. Mellish won't invite him to supper, so we will be under no obligations to the gentleman."

That was it! Mr. Carroll didn't care to have his student frequent the house of Joshua Mellish. He didn't like Mellish, didn't approve of him. Jared's lips curled, and his eyes were very angry. He had thought of telling Mr. Carroll about the man in brown and his quarrel with him, but now he was glad he hadn't. He would tell Mr. Carroll nothing. In the office he would obey the lawyer, but outside he would do as he chose. And that meant he would go to Bellevue—and the more eagerly because Mr. Carroll would disapprove.

VI

THE PARTY AT BELLEVUE

MR. CARROLL'S conduct in sending the money to Mademoiselle de Severac by a hired messenger rankled in Jared's mind. Mr. Carroll should have understood that his student took a personal interest in that business. The graceful thing, the gallant thing, would have been for him to allow Jared to present the money in person. But Mr. Carroll was neither graceful nor gallant; he thought only of the law and its decorum; he was intensely mulish and stupid.

On several occasions during the past winter Mr. Carroll had dropped hints that were intended to guide Jared's conduct, and sometimes Jared had acted on the hints and sometimes he had not. Now, however, he felt that the time had come to assert his independence. The mere fact that Nathaniel Carroll and Jared's father were old friends was no reason why a young fellow should permit himself to be led by the nose by an old fogey. Mr. Carroll didn't like Joshua Mellish; here then was an excellent opportunity for Jared to show that he was his own master.

He was, therefore, in an extremely receptive frame

of mind when, three days later, Norroy invited him
to go to Bellevue. Jared was on his way home to
Mrs. Bird's in the late afternoon when he met the
Englishman. Norroy greeted him warmly.

"You need amusement, my son. Your brow is
pale with much study. What will you give me if
I furnish you with entertainment to drive away
dull care?"

"My hearty thanks," Jared responded, his spirits
rising, as they always did, at meeting this merry
fellow.

"Thanks? Well, thanks are scarcely currency of
the realm, but coming from you I'll accept them as
sufficient payment. Tonight is to be a gala night
at Mellish's house in the country. 'Tis Saturday
evening. I take it you have no objection to allowing Saturday's entertainment to trespass on the
Sabbath?"

"None whatever."

"It will be a merry party. Meet me with your
horse at the tavern on Second Street at seven o'clock.
Array yourself in your best. And don't forget to
slip such notes and coins as you can lay your hands
on in your pockets. Mellish is fond of cards."

Jared nodded. "As you say, Hal. But suppose
we fall in with the highwayman? You remember
the two brothers from Chadd's Ford."

"You and I," said Norroy, "can hold an army

of ruffians at bay. I always carry a pistol when I'm abroad in the country after dark. Dismiss such vile fears, Jared. At seven then, my cock o' the walk!''

With his malacca cane thrust up under his arm he went on along the street.

Jared wasted but little time over the supper Mrs. Bird had prepared for him—he knew there would be plenty to sustain his appetite at Mellish's—and, climbing to his chamber, dressed with the greatest care. His wardrobe was not extensive, but his fawn-colored coat and breeches and black satin waistcoat with pearl buttons were new and in the mode. He unlocked his trunk, took out his pistol, and filled his purse with all the coins it would hold. He might come from the country, but he meant to play his part with the best of the young bloods. Joshua Mellish and his guests should see that Jared Lee was no mere drudge of a clerk.

On the stroke of seven, astride his mare, he met Norroy at the City Tavern, and they took the road out of town. Norroy was in the gayest humor; he told of his recent adventures and it seemed to Jared that his friend led the most delightful existence, his occupation always being to find what should amuse him most. This, Jared fancied, might be partly due to Norroy's having been brought up as a nobleman in England, with wealth enough and to spare; it was also in large measure due to his sanguine, easy-going

nature, which was unvexed by the petty ambitions
and restraints of other young men.

Norroy sang on the country road, and his society
was so entertaining that Jared was surprised to find
them so speedily at the entrance to Bellevue and
picking their way up the winding drive.

A turn showed them the big house, blazing with
lights. A groom, on the lookout for guests, took
their horses. They went up the front steps and into
the hall, where, as it chanced, at the moment Mellish
himself was standing.

"Ah, it's Hal!" said the host, his voice expressing
great pleasure. "And you've brought Mr. Lee with
you. I'm right glad to see you, sir."

He shook hands with Jared, then with Norroy.
"You know where to leave your hat, Hal, and to
find water and such things. Don't dally too long
over your toilet; there are bright eyes waiting
for you."

Jared, when he entered the drawing-room with
his friend, found it vastly more magnificent than
on his first visit. A row of chandeliers, glittering
with wax-lights, was reflected in long mirrors at
the ends and sides of the room, and in mirrors set
in the doors, which gave the effect of illimitable distance. The curtains, the paintings, the furniture,
were bathed in the soft, brilliant glow, which brought
out all the beauty of their color and texture. And

in this setting were grouped ladies and gentlemen costumed in every hue of the rainbow.

"A fine picture, truly!" murmured Norroy, surveying the scene with a gleam in his eye.

Jared nodded. Now that he had taken in the brilliance of the room he was looking for a particular person.

A lady in yellow beckoned with her fan to Norroy, and with a bow he approached her.

Jared, assuming an air of unconcern, skirted a group in the centre of the room and presented himself before Mademoiselle de Severac, who was talking to a man in olive green.

The girl looked up, and a smile parted her lips. "Good-evening, Master Lee."

Jared made his best bow. "Mademoiselle, my respects."

There was a moment's hesitation, then Jeanne turned to the other man. "Colonel Ramsay, are you acquainted with Mr. Lee?"

"I have not had the honor," was the formal response. Jared found himself bowing again, this time to a military-looking man with keen eyes and thin lips.

"Colonel Ramsay has been telling me about the surrender of Yorktown," said Jeanne; "he was there, on General Washington's staff."

"Our French allies were invaluable," declared the

Colonel. "Not alone because of the actual physical aid they gave us, but because of that spirit of gallantry and courage that is characteristic of the whole French people."

Jeanne's face dimpled with pleasure. "Ah, monsieur, you make me very proud! You Americans are so generous in your opinion of us."

"I speak only of what I have observed for myself," Colonel Ramsay answered. "Others will bear the same testimony. For the present I leave that pleasure to Mr. Lee." With a courtly inclination of the head he moved on to another group.

Jared, his eyes fixed on the girl, watched her glance roam over the room. In spite of his unconcerned bearing, he felt oddly diffident. "Mr. Carroll's messenger brought you the money for your necklace?" he finally blurted out.

"Yes, thank you. I am deeply indebted to Mr. Carroll and you."

"I had intended, mademoiselle, to bring you the money myself. To my surprise and regret, when I returned to the office, I found that Mr. Carroll had sent it by another."

"It was a matter of business, Master Lee. And now it is most satisfactorily finished. It is very gay here, isn't it? My father is enjoying himself. But I—sometimes I find myself wishing we hadn't left the Green Anchor."

6

Jared was about to ask her reason for that wish when he saw Jeanne looking beyond him and, turning, he found Cornelius Skipworth and Norroy coming toward them. Skipworth bowed to Jeanne and presented Norroy.

"I recall myself to Mademoiselle de Severac's recollection," said Norroy, "as the man who had the good fortune on Prune Street to direct her to Mr. Carroll's office."

"I remember," laughed Jeanne.

"Thereby," Norroy continued, "securing for Mr. Jared Lee the pleasure of an introduction he had been coveting ever since his eyes fell on the lady in the chaise."

Skipworth touched Jared's arm as the other two fell into conversation. "Glad to see you again," he said. "Hal tells me he brought you. Our good Joshua is in fine fettle tonight. He's been waiting his chance to show his friends that he has a real Marquis under his roof. No doubt it impresses some. At least they know Joshua's whims well enough to let him think they are impressed." Skipworth smiled, his hooded eye glinting at Jared. "What do you say, Mr. Lee, to a game of cards?"

There was a superciliousness about the dandy that made Jared flush. To decline the invitation seemed to him an admission that he was not Skipworth's equal as a sportsman. So he answered coolly, "I'm entirely agreeable."

Guests were now seated at tables in the drawing-room and in a smaller apartment that opened out from the larger one. The groups had broken up, only a few were indulging in tête-à-têtes in chairs along the walls. The real business of the evening was in progress, card playing for stakes, an amusement that was frowned upon by the more respectable element in Philadelphia society, but which reigned supreme among Joshua Mellish's friends.

Jared found himself playing quadrille with Skipworth and two other men at a table in the smaller room. He knew the game, but he recognized that his associates were all far more familiar with it than was he. He had no intention of showing himself outclassed, however; he assumed the air of an old hand, and agreed readily to the stakes that Skipworth proposed. And the Goddess of Chance smiled on him, as she not infrequently does on the reckless beginner, and he discovered himself winning, losing a little, gaining his losses back again, and winning more and more.

He liked to win, of course, but what delighted him the most was the feeling that his luck was irritating and annoying Skipworth, whose manner grew more frigidly polite the longer the game continued. And it was Skipworth who finally said he had had enough.   The other players assented, and Jared nonchalantly thrust his winnings into his pockets.

He went back to the drawing-room feeling that he was a very fine fellow.   He caught a glimpse of Mr. Mellish playing at one of the tables, and was amused to see how intent the host was on his game. At the farther end of the room the Marquis was talking to a stout lady.   In a corner Norroy, seated close to Jeanne, was whispering to her.

Jared went up to them, proud of his triumph over Skipworth.   "Beware, mademoiselle," said he; "Mr. Norroy is a dangerous man."

The two looked up.   "How now, Jared?" said Norroy.   "Has Cornelius let you so early from his clutches?"

"It was he, not I, who called a halt," Jared answered?"

"Mr. Skipworth plays a great deal," said Jeanne. "He showed me some of the finer points of piquet yesterday.   We didn't play for money, only for almonds."

"We played for gold pieces tonight," stated Jared.

"And you plucked him?" exclaimed Norroy. "Aye, I see you did.   There's the winner's glitter to your eye."

"Perhaps Mr. Lee plays a great deal too," Jeanne suggested.

"Perhaps he does," Norroy agreed. "He is, without doubt, a sporting gentleman. I see a man rising from Mr. Mellish's table, and our good host casting his eye about in search of a fresh victim. With your permission, mademoiselle, I will offer myself."

Jared sat down in the chair Norroy had vacated. "Mr. Skipworth stays here too?" he asked. "I suppose you see a great deal of him?"

"Mr. Mellish seems very fond of him," Jeanne answered. "He talks very well, and is always amusing. I think Mr. Mellish likes to have amusing people about him."

"Mr. Mellish is like a king holding court tonight," said Jared. "Don't you care for cards?"

"I play very little. I should disgrace myself with all these accomplished people. And I shouldn't want to lose any of my precious five hundred dollars."

"Of course not," Jared agreed. "Mr. Carroll's daughters, Elizabeth and Hannah, are very inquisitive about you. Hannah in particular has asked me a hundred questions concerning the French lady."

"I should like to meet them," said Jeanne. "I thought Mr. Carroll a charming gentleman."

"Yes." Jared's assent was not altogether wholehearted. "But I don't believe you'd find the Carrolls' society as entertaining as that of Mr.

Mellish and his friends. They belong to the old-fashioned set, and have very fixed ideas as to what is right and wrong. I don't think they'd approve of some of the people here, and I'm sure that most of Mr. Mellish's guests would find the parties of the Carrolls' set unutterably stupid."

"You like the gayer society, don't you?"

"To be sure I do. I like men like Hal Norroy, I like glitter and sparkle, the group at the City Tavern, where we sometimes sit until daylight, I like a game of chance—" He laughed, and added: "In short, I think I like almost everything that Mr. Carroll wouldn't approve of."

Jeanne looked at him questioningly. "So much of this is entirely new to me—and strange," she said. "I have lived very quietly in the country, and except on my visits to England when I was a little girl, and once or twice when I went to Paris, the people I have met have all been of the same type, quiet people like my father. They were not very gay, as the people here are. I—I don't feel altogether at home here at Mr. Mellish's."

Jared noticed a troubled frown in her eyes. "You said you sometimes wished you hadn't left the Green Anchor. Don't you feel secure here? If there were any one threatening harm to you or your father, you would be much better protected from them here than at a public tavern."

"Oh, it's not that any one's threatening us," Jeanne answered quickly, and Jared concluded that Sebastien hadn't told her about the man in brown. "I can't explain—sometimes I wonder if the people here who seem so well disposed toward us are really our friends. Mr. Skipworth, for instance; he laughs at everybody; he puzzles me."

"Oh, Mr. Skipworth—" began Jared, and stopped, biting his lip; he didn't like the dandy, but he wasn't going to express his feeling about him to Jeanne.

The doors to the dining-room were now thrown open, and the guests forsook the card tables for supper. There were refreshments of every kind, from meats to suit the hunger of the heartiest man to candied delicacies to tempt the palate of the most fastidious lady. And the wines were no less varied. The cellars of Bellevue were famous, and from them flowed a prodigal stream of Burgundy and claret, Madeira and port. Servants kept replenishing the tables with fresh platters of fowl and ham and mounds of jellies and puddings.

Jared, introduced by Mr. Mellish to a number of the guests, moved from one group to another. He had a glass of claret with the Marquis, who seemed to Jared, in spite of his sober black, the most distinguished figure there. With Norroy, and a circle of gentlemen, he drank the celebrated Bellevue punch, a beverage calculated to loosen the tongue and make one laugh loudly.

Word got abroad that Jared had won money from Skipworth, and he was complimented. Skipworth, it appeared, was a seasoned gambler, and to better him was accounted quite an achievement. A lady, wearing many jewels, invited Jared to play piquet with her in a secluded corner, and he lost almost all his money. He didn't begrudge her the coins, he could be a gallant loser.

Presently he rose from the card table and went to look for Jeanne. He found her, with her father, about to leave the drawing-room. "Oh, mademoiselle," he exclaimed, "the hour is early! Why hasten away?"

She smiled at him, but shook her head. "The hour is not early for us. My father is tired, and I must go with him to his room. Good-night, Master Lee."

"You will come back again?"

"Not tonight. Two guests will not be missed among so many."

With her hand on her father's arm she turned away, and from the door into the hall Jared watched the two ascend the wide staircase.

His face was flushed with the warmth of the rooms, and, wanting cooler air, he crossed to the open door and going down the steps walked out upon the lawn. As he paced there a man who was also enjoying the freshness of the night came up to him. "I thought it was our young blade from the lawyer's office," said the sarcastic voice of Skipworth, "and so, by Jove, it is!"

Jared turned. "Have you any objection, sir? I may go where I please, I suppose?"

Skipworth regarded him in silence for so long a time that Jared began to chafe.

"You may go where you please, certainly," said Skipworth at last; "but if you don't tread warily, you're likely to lose more than you won from me at cards tonight."

"Are you threatening me, Mr. Skipworth? I don't take threats."

"No, I am merely giving you the benefit of a suggestion. Bellevue and its neighborhood isn't very healthy country for a lawyer's clerk."

"And why not, pray?" Jared was stung by the other's superior manner as much as by his words. "Is it because the lawyer's clerk plays cards too well to suit you?"

"You're insulting," said Skipworth. "I won't bandy words with you." And he turned on his heel.

Jared, however, caught him by the sleeve. "I think it's you who are insulting me," he retorted. "I don't like your manner. I'm Mr. Mellish's guest, not yours; please remember that."

"You fool!" muttered Skipworth, and before Jared knew what he was doing the man had wrenched his sleeve from Jared's fingers and given Jared a blow in the chest with the flat of his hand that almost made him lose his balance. "Now you mind your own manners!" he exclaimed. "Hello, what's this?"

For even as he spoke Jared had made a leap, and now his fist caught Skipworth on the side of the jaw and sent him backward and over, flattened on the grass.

"The score's even," said Jared. "That's in return for your threats." And without waiting for more words he turned and, going into the house, left a message for Norroy with a servant informing him that he had ridden over to the Green Anchor Inn to spend what was left of the night.

VII

RUMORS ALONG THE DELAWARE

It was almost noon when Jared woke, his slumbers being interrupted by a rapping on his door at the inn. "Who's there?" he called out.

"Come and see," said the voice of Norroy, and when Jared unbolted the door it was Norroy who entered, looking as bright and debonair as the spring sunshine.

"Slug-a-bed!" said Norroy. "How can you expect to get on in the world? What says Poor Richard? 'Early to bed, and early to rise, makes a man healthy, wealthy, and wise.' I fear you have not taken the good Doctor Franklin as an example."

"I certainly went to bed early in the morning," laughed Jared. "I suppose you were up betimes and milking the cows."

"When you are as old and wise as I am," the other rejoined, "you will appreciate the beauty of the dew on the grass, the early breeze on the water, the first songs of the birds. To change the subject, Jared, I'm glad you took Skipworth's money."

"Yes, I took it; but I lost it again to a lady." And to find out whether Norroy had heard of his quarrel with the dandy Jared added: "Did you see that gentleman after I left Bellevue?"

"No," answered Norroy. "The servant gave me your message, and I came on here soon after you and procured a room. Joshua has many guest chambers and his neighbors open their houses to his friends, so that none have to drive back to town after his parties. But I prefer a tavern; it's Liberty Hall. Now stir yourself, my boy. I'll tell the innkeeper to send you up hot water. I've breakfasted, and now I'm going out."

So Skipworth had not spoken of their encounter; no, thought Jared, he would not have been likely to, since it had ended in Jared's triumph. But, whatever he had been before, he was now an enemy, and in the sobering light of morning Jared saw that might be a disadvantage.

When the hot water came he bathed and dressed. Descending to the dining-room he found it empty except for a serving-boy.

He ordered a hearty breakfast, for he was hungry, and while he waited for it looked through the window at the broad Delaware, up which a brig was moving. The scene was quiet and peaceful, the Sabbath noon seemed far removed from the revelry of the previous night.

Breakfast eaten, he went out of the inn and walked down to the shore, enjoying the wide reach of blue water and the soft green of the Jersey side. As he was standing, drinking in the picture, the sunlight and the breeze, a man in a rusty green suit, none too clean, a man who smelled of fish, sauntered up and stopped beside him.

"You're from the city?" he said, eyeing Jared's clothes.

Jared gave a nod.

The man regarded him with a rheumy eye and in a speculative manner that amused Jared. "In trade?" the man questioned.

"No; law."

This apparently gave the questioner food for reflection. He thrust his battered hat far back on his head and stared moodily at the river. Jared, waiting a moment, took the next step in the conversation. "Lawyers have to untangle the knots business men make in their affairs."

"I dunno much about lawyers, but if what you say is so they must have an almighty lot to tend to. Was it that kind of business that brought you out here?"

"No," said Jared, "it wasn't." Then, thinking there must be some object in the man's approaching him, he added, "Was there something you wanted to tell me?"

The man squinted behind him, but there was no

one about. "Queer things are happening. I see a lot, I do."

"Are you a sailor?"

"No, I fish for a living. There was a Frenchman here at the inn some days ago."

"I think I know the gentleman you mean. He's staying at Mr. Mellish's now."

"What's a Frenchman doing in these parts? I don't like Frenchmen."

"That," said Jared, "is a matter of taste. This particular French gentleman is doing no harm."

"Isn't he now?" The fisherman's unshaven face became belligerent. "You don't know as much as I do about these furriners."

"Perhaps I don't," agreed Jared in a mollifying tone. "But what harm could he do here in this quiet place?"

"It looks quiet, but you don't know what goes on here sometimes. It ain't only sailors that comes to the inn. No, there be men from the city and men from the country along the Capes, men who have somewhat to tell each other while they drink their ale."

"That's the common business of taverns, isn't it?" Jared said lightly, though he was much interested.

"This is uncommon business," answered the fisherman. "Business that brings gentlemen from the city." He broke off, and again eyed Jared speculatively. "You staying at the inn?"

"Yes," said Jared with a smile. "I'll have to admit that I slept there last night. But my excuse was that I spent the evening at Mr. Mellish's."

"I heard tell o' that. There's little goes on along the river that I don't hear about. That Frenchman now— And there's another furriner been prowling and snooping about here, asking questions and telling no one his business."

"Was he a heavy man in a brown suit of clothes?" asked Jared.

The fisherman nodded. "Know him, do you? Well, I don't like these furriners nosing along the river nor gentlemen telling each other secrets in the tavern there." With a stubborn shake of the head and pulling his battered hat down over his nose, the man sauntered away as casually as he had come up.

Jared smiled to himself. The fisherman was an odd character, probably suspicious of everyone by nature. In this case, however, there might be ground for his suspicions. There was the man in brown, for instance, and there was the highwayman who had held up the two farmers, and Simon Duckett had spoken of privateers that captured innocent merchantmen off the mouth of the river.

Turning back to the inn, he found it wrapped

in Sabbath sobriety.   The gentlemen from Bellevue who had spent the night there had all apparently departed.   Through the window of the public room he saw Oakes napping in a chair.   There was no sign of Norroy, and, concluding that the latter had probably gone over to Mellish's, Jared decided to follow him.

The distance was only a half-mile, and Jared preferred to walk.   There was a footpath along the river, and this gave him an opportunity to watch the small craft that, like gulls, skimmed over the wide stream.   The early afternoon was warm and drowsy, and he was in no haste, so that every once in a while he stopped, dreaming and delighting in the panorama, all so fresh and lucent in its colors after the long winter.

The footpath brought him, through a gate in a hedge of yew, to the front grounds of Bellevue. Across a broad stretch of lawn, which was dotted with flowering shrubs and coppices of small trees, he had a view of the house, a dusky red set off by white trimmings, and looking very capacious.   At some distance, on the opposite side of the front entrance, were the gardens, surrounded by a hedge, and beyond these the greenhouses.   Jared took in the scene with appreciative eyes, and then moved slowly across the lawn toward a little summerhouse, rimmed with lilac bushes in bloom, just inside the gardens.

This side the hedge, however, he stopped. The summerhouse was occupied, he could see a light dress and the coat of a man. Two people were seated on a bench and he knew them at once for Mademoiselle Jeanne and Norroy. The girl, her face in profile, was listening with evident interest to her companion.

Jared drew back to the shade of a maple, and taking off his hat, mopped his forehead with his handkerchief. He suddenly felt very warm. He was also indignant. There was nothing wrong in Norroy's having come over to Bellevue to see Mademoiselle Jeanne and nothing out of the way in her enjoying his company. Yet Jared, for some odd reason, felt angry at them both. Mademoiselle Jeanne was his particular friend, and here was Norroy entertaining her.

Then someone spoke softly behind his back. "Enjoying Joshua's beautiful grounds, Master Lee?"

It was the cool, sarcastic voice of Skipworth, and Jared turned to face him, resentful at being spied on.

"As you see, Mr. Skipworth," he said shortly.

Skipworth apparently had wiped their quarrel and Jared's blow from his mind for he went on imperturbably: "Joshua is very proud of his pleasure-grounds. Here he has a great variety of our native

7

trees, and on the other side of the house are artificial groves composed of trees he has collected from all parts of the world at considerable expense. In the greenhouses are rare plants from the hot climates. And in the gardens you will find a profusion of flowers, as well as a choice gathering of statues representing the celebrated gods and goddesses of ancient Greece, characters that have apparently been greatly admired by the gentility of all eras. The gardens—" His glance shifted toward them. "Ah, I see the summerhouse is occupied."

"So it is," Jared lamely agreed. He felt fairly certain that Skipworth had seen him retreat from the hedge to the maple.

"Mademoiselle Jeanne and Norroy. Our gallant Hal is following up the impression he made last night."

Jared, smoldering with anger at having been caught there, kept a moody silence.

"Norroy is deucedly artful with the ladies," mused Skipworth.

"That sounds like a criticism of him," said Jared, finding something at last that he could lay his tongue to.

"Admiration, not criticism," Skipworth corrected. "I wish I had his talent. His accomplishments are so many that he makes us other men seem like mere country yokels." His voice purred softly and suavely, but his eyes were like pinpricks as they played over Jared's face.

Country yokel! There was something for Jared to resent. "I hadn't observed that myself," he answered. "As for Norroy, he's not perfection. There are stories about him. If he is an English nobleman, as some people say, why doesn't he acknowledge it? No one would think the worse of him for having a title, whereas this way—if he is practising a deception—it makes one wonder at the reason."

"Yes," said Skipworth, "it does, doesn't it? Master Lee, for one, is wondering about it."

That reference to himself in the third person, that attitude—as of baiting an inferior—stung Jared's sensibility. "There are others wondering too," he retorted darkly. "Everyone doesn't take a man at his own value as they do here at Mr. Mellish's."

"So? You think Joshua Mellish and the others of us indiscreet? You are patterning your own views after those of the legal Mr. Carroll?"

"I'm patterning after no one, but I intend to judge for myself. It's as well these days to take no one for granted. I met a fisherman today who thought he had good reason to suspect certain men who frequent the Green Anchor, foreigners, Frenchmen he seemed to have especially in mind."

"And Master Lee drank all that in? Frenchmen

this fellow found distasteful, did he? Did he have reference to our Marquis?"

"That is absurd, of course," said Jared. "But his story shows there are men who are asking questions."

"A fisherman!" jeered Skipworth. "Really I had thought better of your judgment than to listen to such folk. Don't, I beg of you, go with any such yarn to Mr. Carroll. It might injure your reputation." And with that he again looked away toward the summerhouse.

Jared fumed. He knew he had been foolish, he regretted what he had said about Norroy; but his self-contempt only added to his dislike of Skipworth.

"My judgment is my own affair," he said stiffly.

"Quite so," was the indifferent answer. "And I would advise you to keep it—so far as it concerns Joshua Mellish's guests, including Norroy—strictly to yourself." Skipworth turned and walked, with his affectedly mincing step, toward the front entrance of the house.

Jared would have given anything at the moment to plant his fist in that withdrawing back, to whirl the fellow about and speak his opinion of him. But with an effort he refrained. If Skipworth ignored their fight of the previous evening Jared couldn't decently renew it now. Again he wiped his face with his handkerchief, and, as nonchalantly as he could, went to the gate into the gardens.

He had no desire to appear to be an eavesdropper, so he made some noise with the wooden latch of the gate as he opened it, sufficient to be heard by the two in the summerhouse, who immediately turned their heads. "Ah, it's Jared!" said Norroy; and Mademoiselle Jeanne smiled a welcome.

Jared's feelings were tremendously mixed. He was still hot with anger at Skipworth who, he suspected, had purposely come upon him to annoy him, and he was put out with himself for having been so foolish as to lose his temper, and he was somewhat annoyed at Norroy for being with Jeanne. Chiefly, however, he was determined to bear himself as a young blood should, and with that thought uppermost he swung off his hat and saluted the lady.

"All paths seem to lead to Mr. Mellish's gardens," he said on the step of the summerhouse.

"All paths lead to the feet of Mademoiselle de Severac," amended Norroy.

Jeanne colored. "What can I say to such pretty speeches?" she asked, her blue eyes raised to Jared. "Alas, I have no such gifts of the tongue as you American gentlemen!"

"Jared, as a lawyer, must of necessity have a polished tongue," said Norroy; "but as to mine, I find it frequently halts and stumbles for the right word like a blind beggar."

"What a modest gentleman you are! Or what

a hypocrite!" She turned to him, her glance mocking and amused. "I'll be bound you were never at a loss for the right word in your life!"

"Oh, mademoiselle, you're mistaken!"

And Jared stood there, still on the step, feeling altogether out of the comedy.

Jeanne looked again at him; perhaps she caught something of his feeling from his expression; anyway her smile softened. "Shall we three look at Mr. Mellish's flowers?" she suggested.

"I should enjoy it," said Jared.

"And I should enjoy it too," said Norroy, "but I must have some talk with Mr. Mellish before I return to town." With a bow he left them.

Beside the French girl Jared paced the walks of the gardens, looking at the flowers she pointed out and echoing her admiration of them. But his brow was still moody, and presently she said, "Flowers don't interest you, do they?"

"Oh yes, Mademoiselle Jeanne."

She stopped. "Of what are you really thinking?"

The question and her manner were so abrupt that he was taken by surprise. "I was thinking of Cornelius Skipworth. I met him here this afternoon. I don't like him."

"No, I don't think you would. You two are utterly different."

"I ought not to be so thin-skinned."

The ghost of a smile played about her lips. "It's better than being too brazen. I think Mr. Skipworth is that."

"You don't like him then?"

"I—I distrust him. And since he's such a friend of Mr. Mellish sometimes I distrust Mr. Mellish too. If my father didn't like him so much I'd not stay here another day. You mustn't come here to play at cards again."

"Why not?" he demanded, amazed.

"Because they would take all your money. I shouldn't be saying such things to you, but, Master Lee, these people are not trustworthy, not honorable. They are plotters and schemers. If you come here they'll lead you into trouble."

"Will you leave here and come to Philadelphia? Mr. Carroll and I will find a house where your father and you can stay."

"My father likes it here. Mr. Mellish is more than kind to him. My father would think it foolish of me to want to leave. I can take care of myself. But with you—it is different."

"You mean that I can't take care of myself?" he retorted.

She shook her head. "Not that, exactly. But a young man is apt to be tempted. And he thinks that he must do as his companions do."

He looked into her eyes and read there sincerity

and friendship. "Yes, that is true," he conceded. "We are like a flock of sheep."

"Don't you be," she said.

Jared mused a moment. "There is Hal Norroy. He doesn't follow any one's lead."

"Yes," said Jeanne. "He is very attractive." Her eyes looked past him at the golden west. "But Mr. Norroy lives only in the present."

Jared nodded. He understood. Norroy was without ambition, he had no career to make.

Thereupon the French girl turned and walked along the path between two rose-beds in the direction of the house, while Jared, all his ill-humor flown and a new seriousness in his face, strode alongside her.

It was Jeanne who first broke the silence. "You comprehend, I hope, why I spoke so freely. I wanted to speak to you as a sister might, because it appeared to me that you were troubled."

There was a healing balm in her words, and a sudden sense of purposefulness came upon him, a desire to achieve something that should be worth while.

"You are very good to me, mademoiselle; far more so than I deserve."

"It was nothing, an impulse. You are the only person I have spoken to in this way."

He unlatched the gate and they passed through.

Quietly they crossed the broad lawn to the front of the house.

"You will let me know if at any time I can serve you, Mademoiselle Jeanne?" he asked when they were at the steps.

"Gladly," she answered. "I have my father and Sebastien, but I doubt sometimes if I have any other real friends here."

"Tell me," he said, "is there any one—any one in particular who you think might do you harm?"

She shook her head. "No. Only since that night in France I—I— No, I'll not say more."

He watched her go into the house, and when he turned he was wondering if something of the peril that had beset her in France was following her here. As he walked down the drive he threw back his shoulders and doubled up his fists. He would protect Mademoiselle Jeanne and her father while they were in America; that should be his mission, not quarrelling with Skipworth nor losing money at cards. It seemed as if some high good fortune had given him, Nathaniel Carroll's law student, real man's work to do.

VIII

ADVENTURE ON THE ROAD

In such a mood of high endeavor Jared, as the sun was westering, took his way to the Green Anchor Inn, and had nearly come there when a man, who was following a path across a field that converged in the road, accosted him.

"Good-evening," said the man. "Fine day, sir."

"Fine," agreed Jared. "Excellent weather for farming."

The stranger nodded. He was a young man, of a strong, wiry build, not very tall, but deep-chested, and with long arms. His head was set solidly on his shoulders and his shirt, which was open in front, displayed a massive throat. His face was good-humored, but his nose was crooked to one side, as if it had at some time been dented by a blow. There was also a scar along the line of his jaw, which did not add to the symmetry of his features. His hair was close-cropped. For the rest he was dressed in a rustic suit of butternut brown.

"You're making for the tavern, I'll venture," said the man. "So be I." And he fell into step.

"This is a quiet stretch of country," said Jared, to be friendly.

106

"Yes, sir, 'tis on a Sunday. Too quiet for my taste." This was accompanied by a chuckle. "That's why I'm going to the tavern for a glass of ale, and some talk over it."

"I know something of farms myself," Jared volunteered. "I was raised on a farm along the Conestoga River at Lancaster. The Conestoga's not so big as the Delaware, but it's a fine place to swim and fish and learn to handle boats."

"So you're from Lancaster?" said the other. "Oh, aye, I've been there. Did you know a man named Jonas Buckley?"

"You mean the one who worked in the smithy? A big, raw-boned fellow with a squint in one eye? Yes, I know him, though I can't say intimately."

"I fought him ten rounds and knocked him out. That was in last September. He's a good un, light on his feet and quick with his hands; but not so quick as I be." The man added with a grin, "I can work my left fist as quick as my right."

"You fought Buckley?" said Jared, with new interest in his companion. "Why, he had a great name as a fighter all through our part of the country. I remember hearing men talk of some of his battles."

"Aye, no doubt. And maybe you'll have heard some of 'em talking of me. My name's Luke Hatch."

"I'm sure I would have if I'd been in Lancaster when you fought the smith," said Jared. "But I was in Philadelphia."

"Yes, sir, I'm Hatch," the other continued; "and I'm always ready to take on a sporting offer. Maybe some of your friends in Philadelphia would like to make a match for me. I'm to be found at the house nearest the first fork in the Chester Road as you go north along the river. I do a bit o' farming, but I'll fight for a proper purse."

The inn, its windows shining with the slanting sun, lay to the left of the road.

"I had a go here once with an English sailor," said Hatch, indicating a stretch of turf to the right of the stables, "and I showed him a thing or two. That was a big day for me, sir. There must have been a couple o' hundred here to see the mill, and they gave me a fat purse. Be you interested in the fancy yourself? I thought you might be when I first laid eyes on you. I says to myself, 'There's a young gentleman as is likely to care for the sport.'"

"I don't know much about your particular kind of sport," Jared said with a smile. "But if I hear of any one who wants to make a match I'll mention your name."

"Thank you, sir. I'd take it as a favor."

Hatch went on to the inn, while Jared stopped at the stables to speak to the hostler about his mare, and then stepped into the tavern. Oakes was in the bar, and Jared asked if his friend, Norroy, had returned. The innkeeper said that he hadn't seen him, adding that he thought all the gentlemen who had come from Bellevue to spend the night had ridden away some time since.

Jared had had but one meal that day, his breakfast at noon, and now he was feeling hungry. So he ordered a good cut of roast beef, some potatoes and greens, and, seeing Luke Hatch drinking a glass of ale at a table by himself, suggested that his meal should be served there.

Hatch was glad of his company. This fighting farmer drank his ale with relish, but wagged his tongue with even more delight. " 'Tain't good to eat alone, sir," he said, as Jared drew up his chair. "Talk helps the juices. To my way of thinking a tavern's a wonderful thing. These here country roads would be mighty lonely if there wasn't a tidy bar now and then to brighten 'em up a bit."

The roast beef and vegetables came, and Jared ordered a tankard of beer, and a fresh one for his companion.

"Are you going to town tonight?" Hatch asked presently.

Jared nodded.

"The road to the north's safe to travel," said the

prize-fighter; "but I've heard stories of robberies in the country south of here."

"So have I," said Jared. "I met two farmers from Chadd's Ford one night who'd been robbed on the other side of the fork. But they had a considerable sum of money with them, and I think the robber knew it. Such men don't waste their time picking empty purses." He smiled across the table. "My purse, as it happens, is as flat as a pancake."

" 'Tis the best way to travel," said Hatch. "There are strange men in the river country. I pick up a bit o' gossip now and then, and I know there are more than law-abiding farmers between here and Lewes."

"Why don't you and your neighbors clean them out?" Jared demanded.

Hatch winked and laid a finger alongside his crooked nose. "What's everybody's business is nobody's business," he answered. "If a man tries to do me harm I defend myself; but I don't go a-hunting trouble." He drank and wiped his lips with the back of his hairy hand. " 'Tain't my affair, no sir! But I've been down through the country to Lewes—I had a fight there last April—and I've seen men who wouldn't tell what their business was. I didn't ask them, I knew they wouldn't explain."

"Privateer crews?" Jared suggested, lowering his voice.

"You might call them that, or you might call them anything else. The main thing is they don't talk about their business. When a man won't do that, I know there's some good reason. But it ain't my affair, sir, any more than I reckon it's yours."

Jared nodded and pushed away his empty plate. "My immediate concern is to get back to town." He rapped on the table, and, when Oakes came, paid his bill. "If my friend, Mr. Norroy, calls here for me, tell him I started homeward," he directed the innkeeper. Rising, he put on his hat.

"You won't forget Luke Hatch, if any of your friends are making up a match?" urged the prize-fighter.

"No, I won't forget," laughed Jared. "Good-night."

The roan was saddled and ready in the stable-yard. Jared gave the hostler a coin, mounted, and rode off.

He had sat so long at the table that twilight had faded into night. The sky was full of stars, the breeze soft and perfumed. He trotted along, his thoughts repeating the talk he had had with Jeanne in the gardens. They were pleasant thoughts, and inspiring; far more interesting to him than the fences, fields, bushes, and occasional woods that lay along the highroad. His pistol was in his coat, but he felt no special concern for highwaymen. As he had told Hatch, his purse was empty and not worth the picking.

He came to the fork and noted absently the low-lying cottage that Luke Hatch had described as his farmhouse. He went on, around a curve where woods hid the view, and suddenly found himself jerking his mare to a standstill. Ahead of him, in the middle of the road, was a horseman in a black vizor and a long, enveloping cloak.

Jared had his pistol out in a flash, but he had no more than aimed it when there was a spat of fire in the darkness and a bullet sped so close to his horse's nose that the roan reared on her hind legs. At the same moment he fired, but the roan's leap caused his bullet to fly into the trees.

"Drop your pistol," said the masked man, "or I'll shoot your horse!"

The roan was plunging now; Jared gripped his legs about her. His purse was empty; the highwayman would shoot his horse; his opponent had the advantage of a steady seat and had drawn a second pistol from under his cloak. To save the mare Jared let his firearm fall to the ground.

The man in the vizor rode nearer, still keeping Jared covered, while Jared quieted the roan and brought her to a standstill. He grinned as he thought what poor plucking the man would find him.

"Have you other arms?" the highwayman demanded.

"No," answered Jared.

"I'll see," was the response. He stuck his spare pistol back in his belt and his gauntletted hand ran over Jared's coat and breeches, wherever a weapon might be.

"Now," said the man, "sit still."   And with his firearm aimed at the roan's head he swung down from his saddle, snatched up the pistol Jared had dropped and was up on his mount again in one swift movement. "Give me your purse," he ordered.

"You're welcome to it," Jared retorted. "It's empty." He pulled his purse from his coat pocket and thrust it toward the robber.

The highwayman stuck the purse under his cloak. For a moment he toyed with his pistol while his eyes, behind the mask, regarded Jared. "If the purse is empty, as you say, we'll make up for that by adding the horse to it. Get down." And he laid his hand on the roan's bridle.

Jared ground his teeth. This was more than he had bargained for. It flashed through his mind to dig heels in the mare and dash away from the robber, taking a chance of a bullet.

"Down!" came the order, and the muzzle of the highwayman's pistol was thrust against Jared's chest.

Perforce Jared slid down from the roan, vowing

8

to himself he would even matters up with this bandit some fine day.

No sooner were his feet on the ground than the highwayman jerked the mare's head about, and, holding her by the rein, started off down the road in the direction from which Jared had come.

A voice boomed out from somewhere. "Loose that horse or I'll send a bullet through you!"

The masked man looked over his shoulder and seeing that the speaker intended to do what he said dropped the rein and, swinging away from the roan, bent low in his saddle and dug his spurs in his own horse.

Jared, amazed, looked up as a second horseman thundered from the north. An instant later he exclaimed, "Hal Norroy!"

The rider, who was in fact Norroy, reined up sharply. "Did he get anything from you but your horse?" he asked.

"He took my purse, with a few silver pieces, and my pistol. Never mind them, Hal. The mare is safe."

Norroy grunted. For a moment he appeared undecided. Then he slipped his pistol back into his coat. "I'll not waste good lead on him, Jared, though I was mightily tempted. You've got your horse. Whistle to the roan, and let's be on our way."

Overjoyed at this swift turn of fortune Jared

mounted his mare and rode up to his friend. "By all that's wonderful, Hal!" he exclaimed; "how did you come to be here?"

"Providential, wasn't it, Jared? I'm a thoughtless fellow, but yet I have a conscience. I rode to Bellevue this noon, and after I surrendered the French mademoiselle to you in the gardens I went to the house to see Mellish. He had some men there, and I stayed to supper with them, and later rode with one of them to his house up the river toward town. Then, when I took the highroad tonight, something whispered to me that I hadn't done my duty by you. Here was I, who had taken you to Bellevue, abandoning you to possible mischances. My conscience commenced to stir." Norroy looked at the youth riding alongside him. "You didn't think I had a conscience, did you, Jared? That's not my reputation, I know."

Jared patted the velvet neck of his mare, and laughed in high good humor.

"I haven't a conscience where most people are concerned," said Norroy. "But I seem to have one concerning you; attributable probably to the fact that since you are studying law I regard you as having no knowledge of practical affairs. As I say, my conscience chid me. There was I, armed, and used to fighting; there were you, brave, but unaccustomed to dealing with rascals. My conscience tugged at the reins, and behold I came flying back! I saw you standing in the road. I saw a man riding off with your horse. And you know the rest."

"I'm right glad you have a conscience, Hal!" chuckled Jared. "I should have hated to lose this trusty mare of mine."

"The infernal villain!" said Norroy. "To take a gentleman's horse! He's a most ill-bred knave!"

"What do you expect of a robber?"

"Aye," said Norroy, "what does one expect of such? Well, my lad, all's well that ends well. And now tell me, what do you think of our friend Joshua's celebrated entertainments?"

"Rather too rich food for Mr. Carroll's student," Jared answered with a smile.

"I shouldn't wonder if you were right. And the little French lady—she's too fine for the company she's in."

"I agree with you," said Jared. "I wish she and her father would come to Philadelphia."

"Hm—m," considered Norroy. "Mellish has taken a great liking to the Marquis, and we don't want to displease Joshua."

"I wouldn't care how much I displeased him, or Cornelius Skipworth either!" was the quick rejoinder.

Norroy glanced at his companion. "You're at odds with Skipworth, are you?"

"He insulted me last night and I knocked him down."

Norroy whistled. "So? So? Aha, I begin to understand matters!" Then he shook his head. "No, no, Jared, it won't do. If you've made an enemy of Cornelius you've got to keep away from Bellevue. He's a snake in the grass, and he'll sting you if he gets the chance."

"Let him try it, Hal!"

"No. Brave words don't mend broken bones, Jared. See, yonder are the lights of the ferry. I'm glad to get such a fighting-cock as you safely home."

"Hal, you know more about this highwayman and the plots that are going on along the river than you've told me."

"Maybe I do, Jared. But ask me no questions and I'll tell you no lies. I helped you tonight, didn't I?"

"I'm very much in your debt. But now that I've got my horse I shall ride to Bellevue some day and get even with that highwayman if I meet him on the road!"

IX

THE MAN IN BROWN

JARED was kept busy on work for Mr. Carroll most of the next day. When he left the office late in the afternoon he saw Hannah and her elder sister Elizabeth talking with a young man on the brick walk before their front door. At the same time Elizabeth caught sight of him and waved a beckoning hand. Elizabeth was nineteen, a tall and pretty girl, much more attractive to Jared than her younger sister, so he gave her an answering nod and smile and strolled over to the three.

The girls' companion was their cousin, Thomas Clayton, a round-faced fellow with straw-colored hair, who considered himself a man of society, and was proud of his intimate knowledge of all that was going on. " Ah, Jared," he said. " And what have you been doing lately? Frequenting the taverns? Or do you spend your evenings in study of the law?"

"Frequenting the Green Anchor Inn perhaps," suggested the irrepressible Hannah, fixing Jared with her bold brown eyes.

Elizabeth saw him flush and came to the rescue. "Master Jared is wiser than some people I know of," she said. "He doesn't prate of everything he does."

"He certainly hasn't told us much of his French Marquis and his daughter," Hannah put in quickly. "Have you heard about them, Tom?"

"Why, no," said Clayton, "I don't think I have."

"If Tom hasn't heard of them," said Elizabeth, who liked to tease her cousin, "they can't be of great importance."

"Oh, but they are!" cried Hannah. "The young French lady is very beautiful."

Three pairs of eyes turned to Jared, who assumed an indifferent air. "Since Miss Hannah knows so much about the subject, why should I add anything?" he said.

"But why do they stay at a common country inn," Hannah pursued, "when they might be enjoying themselves in Philadelphia?"

"Why, indeed?" echoed Clayton. "I am sure we would welcome them here."

"Perhaps they don't care for society," said Elizabeth. "Many nice people don't."

Jared, under the inquisitive gaze of Clayton, felt obliged to speak. "If you would know," he said, "the Marquis de Severac and his daughter have left the Green Anchor and are staying at Bellevue, Mr. Joshua Mellish's house."

"Indeed!" chirped Clayton. "At Bellevue!" His expression showed much surprise.

"Mr. Joshua Mellish?" puzzled Hannah. "Have I heard of him?"

"I doubt it," said Clayton, and mused a moment. "Mellish and his circle wouldn't come within your knowledge."

"Oh, Tom," said Elizabeth, "you superior creature! You ought to be ashamed of putting on such airs!"

Clayton's round face showed a deeper pink. "I happen to know considerable about Mellish's house, Elizabeth," he said with dignity.

The insinuation in the words was more than Jared could put up with. He had always thought Thomas Clayton a prig, and now he thought him insulting as well. "Mr. Mellish's country home is one of the most elegant to be found anywhere," he stated warmly, "and his guests are the most attractive people."

"You're acquainted there, are you?" said Clayton in a tone of amazement.

Jared bowed. "I had the honor of attending a party at Bellevue no longer ago than last Saturday night."

The two girls were now very much interested. Evidently Jared Lee moved in a circle with which they were unfamiliar, a circle of which their cousin apparently didn't approve.

"In that case I've nothing to say," responded Clayton, shifting his gaze from Jared's hostile face.

"That's fortunate," said Jared, deigning to smile. He turned to Elizabeth. "Bellevue is a charming place, and the Marquis and his daughter have made many friends."

"I'm glad to hear it," said Elizabeth. "But I do hope they will come to see us."

"I shall urge them to," said Jared; and with a bow to the two girls he walked away. He was glad he had spoken as he had to Clayton, and yet he knew that Clayton's opinion of Mellish and his friends was not unjustified.

In search of more information about the lawlessness along the Delaware he went that evening down to the riverfront, and, as he hoped, found Simon Duckett smoking an after-supper pipe on a bench he had brought out from his shop and placed in front of his door.

"Good-evening, Simon," said Jared. "Are you dreaming of the high seas, or figuring your profit on the last bill of goods you sold to Stephen Girard?"

"Sit you down," responded the little chandler, making room for Jared beside him on the bench. "I've been watching the sailors and trying to pick out the country from which each hails. My wife

is upstairs, putting the youngsters to bed.   It's a
time of calm after a lively squall."

"It's calm enough here along the docks tonight,"
said Jared, "but I've been down in the south country,
and there's talk of strange men along the river there."

"Aye," said Duckett, "wherever there's a river,
with shipping on it, there's like to be talk of strange
men.   And it's right there should be on the Delaware,
for I've seen a might o' sailors of all races come up
this stream.   And what with war abroad, and the
news from France, a sailor hardly knows what flag
he's sailing under.   You don't have to go down
to the country to hear tell o' such things, Jared.
You can hear 'em wherever the ship-owners and
masters meet in the streets.   A French letter-of-
marque has captured an American merchantman on
the high seas, a Philadelphia ship belonging to Mr.
Wyant.   What with the French and the English,
and some that don't rightly belong to either country,
it's ticklish business sending out an American ship
these days."

Jared nodded.   "It wouldn't be hard, I suppose,
for men to learn the value of the cargoes bound down
the river?"

"It would not," the chandler affirmed.   "If it
was worth my while I could find out for you what's
going aboard every ship at the docks.   And every

other man who's used to the business could do the same. You don't need no spies for that."

"We're such a young country," mused Jared, "that the men of other nations think they can do what they please with us."

"There might be something in that," considered Duckett. "But there's something else too. There's somewhat about the sea itself that makes for lawlessness. Men have made rules about it, of course; but if you break those rules who's any the wiser? And the sailors now......Most of 'em left their homes when they was lads, ran away many of 'em, and homes don't mean anything to them. When a man hasn't got a home he's got nothing to tie to, he's a wanderer, as you might say, and he gets into the habit of doing what comes easiest. And on the sea it's sometimes easiest to take what don't belong to you. There's right-acting sailors, of course; but take 'em as a lot—and I know a deal about 'em—sailors haven't got what you'd call a landsman's conscience."

"You mean they're tempted to turn pirates, Simon?"

Duckett gave a grim smile. "It's an ugly word, Jared; but let me tell you it's often a very small thing that separates an honest sailor from a buccaneer. There's the wide sea—lay your hands on a prize and who's to know what your crew has done?

or to catch you, with a thousand ports where a sailor may hide?"

For a few moments Jared watched the ebb and flow of wayfarers in the street, most of them men who had to do with ships or shipping, an odd, nondescript crew, with clothes of many cuts, and weather-beaten faces that seemed in the dusk of the docks to add point to the chandler's observations.

"And the city merchants are doing nothing to safeguard their ships?" Jared asked presently.

Duckett took his pipe from his mouth. "Nothing, so far as I hear of. Each is after his own gain, and until his pocket is touched he takes it out in talking. There's plenty of speeches made in the counting-houses and at the City Tavern, but when it comes to action—oh, that's a different matter!" He let his hand fall on Jared's knee as he added with a chuckle, "By the Lord, if I was a pirate I'd ask no better picking than these merchants of ours!"

Jared laughed. "I've no doubt you would make a very successful pirate, Simon, if you put your hand to it."

"No doubt I could," was the answer, "and that's no very great compliment to my intelligence either. What with half our people backing the French and t'other half the English there's plenty of opportunity for any one to make goats of us. And they're doing it, lad. There's many a foreigner comes to this town these days, looking for plunder. 'Twas only a few nights ago I met a Frenchman just landed from a ship from Havre."

"Perhaps he was one of the King's party," Jared suggested. "You don't think all Frenchmen who come to our shores are thieves?"

"No, he was none of the Royalists, as they call them," said Duckett. "He told me what the people were doing to the nobles in France, and from the way he spoke I judged he was mightily pleased with it and had taken a share himself in what he called 'the great work.' He spoke pretty fair English for a foreigner, said he'd been to England several times. He wasn't a sailor and he wasn't a farmer; I couldn't make out what his business was." Duckett stopped to pull at his pipe. "But there was a queer look to his eyes that made me think he was up to something evil."

"If he wanted plunder," said Jared, "he'd better have stayed in France. Men of his kind are robbing all the old houses."

"He was looking for someone over here. He didn't speak of it at first, but came around to the subject gradually. I was sitting out here on my bench, and he came up, and passed the time of day. He asked me a good many questions about the city, as if he was trying to find out how much I knew about what was going on. It seems I satisfied him, for presently he says, 'Have you heard tell of a French gentleman, a Marquis, who's lately come over here?' "

"A Marquis?" exclaimed Jared, instantly thinking of the man in brown. "Did he mention the Marquis's name?"

"No," said Duckett. "He told me the Marquis came from his part of France—and that, I figure, must be somewhere near Havre—and that there were reasons why it was important for him to find him. Thinks I to myself, 'There may be important reasons from your point of view, my lad; but I'm not so sure the Marquis would care to see you.' However I told him I'd heard naught of any such Frenchman, but didn't doubt that if he'd make inquiries he could find out where the nobleman lodged. And that was all the talk that passed between us; but, as I say, there was a queer, ratty look to the fellow's eyes."

"Simon," said Jared, "was he a thick-set man in brown clothes?"

"Yes," answered the chandler.

"Then," said Jared, "I've seen him, and I think perhaps I know the nobleman he was looking for. He's not in the city, and I'm sure he wouldn't want to see this man from Havre. He was driven away from his home by just such villains as that, and now that he's here in America he ought to be safe from them."

"Well, I hope he may be," agreed Duckett. "I took no like to the man. Maybe you'll be telling your friend the Marquis about him."

"I don't know," said Jared. "I want him to feel secure here. I'll wait and see. It's not likely the man can do him any harm."

There came a woman's voice from a window on the upper floor, and the chandler knocked out his pipe. "I'm wanted abovestairs, Jared," he said. "This here mate always obeys his captain's orders. Good-night to you, lad."

Jared walked home in thought. If the man in brown had come to threaten the Marquis and his daughter he would find that they had friends in this country: Joshua Mellish at Bellevue, and Mr. Carroll and Jared in Philadelphia.

A few days later Jared, answering a knock at the office door one afternoon, opened it to the Marquis and Jeanne. Sebastien had driven them up to town, the Marquis explained, and they had done some needed shopping. Mr. Carroll welcomed them warmly and took them into his house, where his wife insisted that they must stay to supper. And to Jared's great satisfaction Mrs. Carroll invited him too.

He returned at six, having made a careful toilet,

and found the guests and the Carrolls mutually delighted with each other. Mrs. Carroll was talking to the Marquis, who, in figure and bearing as well as in conversation, had a dignity that would charm the most fastidious lady. Jeanne was recounting her shopping adventures to the lawyer and his daughters, all of whom evidently found the lively French girl vastly entertaining.

Supper was announced by the negro man-servant, and Mrs. Carroll, accepting the arm of the Marquis, led the way to the candle-lit dining-room. Hannah, bringing up the rear with Jared, whispered in his ear, "I don't blame you at all, sir, no, that I don't! She is the prettiest thing!"

Mr. Carroll set a bountiful table, and if there were not so many dishes served as was customary at Bellevue, there were sufficient to satisfy any normal appetite. Jared, glancing now and again across the mahogany at Jeanne, thought he could read what was in her mind: she found the company here more agreeable to her than that at Mellish's.

The Marquis presently said, "I presume, Mr. Carroll, that you are acquainted with our host in the country, Mr. Joshua Mellish? He is a gentleman of the greatest amiability, and, I judge, a horticulturist of mark."

The lawyer took a sip of his prized Madeira, tast-

ing the wine deliberately, as was his wont. "I know
the gentleman," he answered, "but not at all intimately.   His interest in horticulture is news to me;
but it shows a cultivated mind.   He is reputed to
be a man of very large wealth."

"He must be," said the Marquis. "He lives in
a most lavish style."

Mrs. Carroll put in a word.   Glancing at her husband, she asked, "Where did he get his money,
Nathaniel?   I don't think I ever heard."

"Nor I, my dear," said the lawyer. "It's reported
by some that he was uncommonly fortunate in certain shipping ventures, cargoes to the south and the
West Indies.   But that may be mere rumor.   I
know nothing personally of the history of his
wealth.   Mr. Mellish is not a Philadelphian by birth,"
he added to the Marquis, as if to explain his ignorance concerning the owner of Bellevue; "I think he
comes from Maryland, or possibly Virginia."

"They say he gives wonderful parties."   It was
Hannah who spoke, her brown eyes turned to Jeanne.

The French girl smiled. "Ask Mr. Lee," she said.
"He can judge such entertainments far better than I."

"Yes," agreed the Marquis, "Mr. Lee was at
Bellevue, with many other guests from Philadelphia,
at a recent entertainment.   I think he found it to
his taste."

The eyes of all at the table turned to Jared, who
9

found himself much embarrassed by Mr. Carroll's inquiring glance. "Quite to my taste, sir," he said boldly. "I have never seen more lavish hospitality. I've never been to a house so fine as Mr. Mellish's; I doubt if there are any in the city. It is very ornate and—"

"Hm—m," interrupted Mr. Carroll; "your views are interesting, Master Jared. Monsieur de Severac, let me urge you to take another slice of the duck and a fresh glass of Burgundy."

The subject veered away from Mellish, to Jared's great relief. He caught Elizabeth's eye and smiled, and even dared to wink at her. She appreciated the awkwardness of his situation between the Marquis, Mellish's friend, and her father, who evidently didn't like Mellish.

As they waited after supper for Sebastien to drive up in the chaise Jared found an opportunity for a word with Jeanne. "All goes well at Bellevue?" he asked. "I can see that your father is enjoying it there."

"Oh yes," she answered. "He likes everyone who seems to like him. But I wish—more than ever now that we've met the Carrolls—that fortune had brought us to Philadelphia rather than to Bellevue."

Farewells were said, and the chaise drove off. Jared stood on the footway, hat in hand, looking after the carriage. When he turned he saw a man standing not far away under a tree at the corner, and thought he recognized him. He walked up to the man. "What are you doing here?" he demanded.

The man faced about. He was the fellow in the brown suit. With a scowl he said: "Taking the air, that's what I'm doing."

"You were watching Mr. Carroll's visitors. If you try to do them any injury you'll find yourself in jail. We don't want such as you in this country."

"They don't want such as you down the river," retorted the fellow. "You'd better keep in town."

"You stay where you are till I tell you you can go," ordered Jared, and, folding his arms, he stood there on guard until he thought the chaise must have reached the ferry. "Now be off with you before I change my mind and hand you over to the watchman."

The fellow laughed. "I'll show you what's what some of these days, master. I'm in no hurry. And I don't care that—" He gave a loud snap of his fingers. "I don't care that for your fine fat lawyer or for you, Monsieur Simpleton!"

Jared made a motion toward him and the man scuttled off, leering back over his shoulder and muttering in a mixture of French and English.

X

SEBASTIEN COMES TO TOWN

MR. CARROLL, coming into the office next morning, read the slip of paper on which were noted his engagements for the day, and then, pushing his chair back from his writing-table, drew his snuff-box from his pocket and helped himself generously to its contents, an unusual proceeding for him so soon after breakfast.

"Jared," he said, as he flicked the grains of snuff from his coat with a handkerchief.

"Yes, Mr. Carroll." Jared looked up from his book over at his seat by the window.

"Jared, I have been giving some thought to our guests of last evening. They are, in my estimation, very honorable people."

"Yes, sir, I think so too."

The lawyer's face crinkled into a little smile, followed almost at once, however, by a frown. "You may have gathered, from what I have implied on one or two occasions, that I have no very high opinion of their host, Mr. Mellish." Here Mr. Carroll turned his chair about, and with his hands on the arms focussed his direct gaze on the young man by the window.

132

"I have gathered that, sir. Perhaps I should have told you that I'd been to his house, as you heard last night at supper."

"I have no intention of criticizing you, Jared. The Marquis and his daughter are staying there, and I can quite understand your desire to renew their acquaintance. But this man Mellish is not fit company either for our French friends or for you."

"There were a good many reputable people there the evening I went to his party. I think you must know a number of them, sir."

"Reputable? What were they doing?"

This was the direct question, shot out with Nathaniel Carroll's customary force at a witness, and Jared felt obliged to reply. "Many of them were playing at cards."

"For money stakes, of course. Gambling, in short." Mr. Carroll shook his big head. "Gambling is one of the worst of vices in its effect on character. With that passion in his blood a man— or a woman—will not hesitate at crime to obtain the means to satisfy his desire. Statesmen have been wrecked by it, and if you go into the prisons you will be surprised to find how many of the inmates owe their situation there to the lust for games of chance. No, Jared, a young man may say it is but a passing folly, the sport of the moment, the fashion of his set; but indeed it is far other than that, it has tentacles, like the octopus.   A gambler—respectable?—No, no; respectability flies from such."

There was a few moments' silence, while Mr. Carroll's gaze, travelling away from Jared, seemed to dwell on pictures of moral turpitude.   Then he resumed.   "You say there were a good many reputable people at Mellish's card tables, and that you think I must know a number of them.   I daresay there were people of excellent family connections and that I am acquainted with some—my acquaintance is wide and includes some black sheep.   But Mellish has turned his house into what would be called in vulgar parlance a gambling hell.   And what of the man who does that?   What shall we say of him?   What of him who invites young men to his house and invites them to play?"   The lawyer dropped his voice, a trick that was an instinct with him in closing his case to a jury.   "Is such a man a fit character to harbor a girl like Mademoiselle Jeanne?"

"I think she shares some of your own opinions, sir," said Jared.   "She would like to get away."

"She and her father must leave there," said Mr. Carroll.   "But my thoughts at the moment have a wider range.   I knew something of Mellish, and since my talk with the Marquis last evening I know more.   He is a sore that festers in our Philadelphia

society. Isn't there some way in which we may
be rid of him?"

"He seems open-handed and above-board, sir.
He seems to have no objection to all the world
knowing what he does."

"He seems—yes...." Mr. Carroll mused, making his sucking sound with his pursed lips. "There
have been rumors and strange stories along the river
this spring."

"You've heard them? I've heard them too, at
the Green Anchor Inn."

"The merchants are uneasy. A client of mine
was urging me yesterday to see if the government
could be induced to give greater protection to our
shipping. Several ships are reported to have been
seized by privateers. But there's constant bickering,
and the clashing of opposing interests, those who
favor the English and those who laud the French;
and meantime—.... When honest men fall out—
Well, then's the time for the Devil to play his
game." Mr. Carroll bent forward. "Jared, I believe there are men in this country, yes, in this very
city, who are making money out of our merchants'
misfortunes."

"You mean men who are taking advantage of
the unsettled conditions to do some privateering on
their own account?" Jared asked, intensely interested.

"That's one way of stating it. What they are

actually doing isn't clear to me—if it was I'd be acting, and not talking about it—but there's under-hand work somewhere. You go about the city, you meet young men at the taverns, you have friends along the river; I thought you might gain information more readily than I."

This suggestion was to Jared's liking. "I shall keep my ears open, sir," he assured the lawyer. "And I have several friends who are well informed of what goes on; they may be useful too."

"We must clear our Augean stables," said Mr. Carroll, and turning about picked up a quill and began to write a letter.

Three days passed, and then, in the afternoon, Mr. Carroll being absent from the office, Jared answered a knock at the street door and Sebastien, the Marquis's servant, came into the room. He had ridden up from Bellevue and was hot and dusty. Jared pushed a chair forward, and Sebastien gratefully sat down.

"I have a message for you, sir, from Mademoiselle Jeanne," he stated in excellent English.

"For me?" said Jared eagerly.

"Mademoiselle Jeanne's instructions were to give it to no one else."

Jared smiled, while Sebastien thrust his hand into the side pocket of his snuff-colored coat.

The hand came out again, empty. The elderly

servant's face had a puzzled expression. He unbuttoned his coat and felt in an inside pocket. He picked up his hat from the floor and looked in the lining. Again his hand went into his side pocket.

He stood up, pressing his hand over his coat and breeches. Finally he said, "The message was in my pocket, in an envelope; but it's gone, sir!"

"You're sure you put it in your pocket?" asked Jared.

"I'm certain of that, Mr. Lee." Again Sebastien searched every part of his clothes where a letter might possibly be carried; but no envelope was forthcoming.

"Could it have dropped out on your ride?" asked Jared.

Sebastien shook his head. "I don't see how it could, sir. That pocket is deep."

"Tell me what you've been doing," said Jared.

"I've ridden straight to your door from the Green Anchor Inn, Mr. Lee."

"From the inn? Not from Mr. Mellish's?"

"From the inn, sir. Mademoiselle Jeanne called me to her room at Mr. Mellish's and gave me this letter, saying I was to hand it to you and to no one else, not even to Mr. Carroll. She didn't want any one to know she was sending you the message, and so she directed me to go to the inn and hire a horse there. That was what I did, sir; I got a horse at the inn."

"Sit down," said Jared, noticing how tired and worried Sebastien looked. "Now let's try to find out what happened. You took the letter from Mademoiselle Jeanne and put it in the side pocket of that coat you have on and went directly to the inn. What did you do there?"

"I spoke to the hostler at the stables about a horse, and while he was saddling him I stepped into the taproom for a small glass of brandy."

"Did you talk to any one there?"

"Only a word to Mr. Oakes about the brandy. There were two other men in the room, sitting at a table."

"Did you know these two men?" Jared asked.

"No, Mr. Lee. But they went out to the stables when I did, and spoke to the hostler and to me. They wanted to know where I was riding, and I said I had business in Philadelphia."

"And did either of them come up close to you, close enough, for instance, to have put his hand in your side pocket?"

Sebastien looked bewildered. "They might have, sir," he said hesitantly. "They had horses of their own there, and they moved about while they talked. I looked at the straps of my saddle and such matters. They might have come close enough."

"After you put Mademoiselle Jeanne's letter in your pocket at Bellevue did you feel in your pocket again until you looked for the letter here just now?"

"No, sir."

"And you came directly here, without stopping to talk to any one on the road?"

The crestfallen Sebastien nodded. "I ought to have ridden with my fingers on Mademoiselle Jeanne's letter," he said distressfully.

Jared took a turn up the room. "If you had it in your pocket when you left Bellevue and it didn't drop out on the road—and I don't see how it could have—someone must have taken it from your pocket. And who could have done that but one of the men at the Green Anchor stables?"

"But why, Mr. Lee? Why would any one want to steal Mademoiselle Jeanne's message to you?"

Jared stopped before the puzzled servant. "I don't know. But you said that Mademoiselle Jeanne didn't want any one to know she was sending me the message. Have you any notion what was in her thoughts?"

Sebastien stared at the floor, the fingers of his right hand plucking at a leather button on his coat. "I think she wants your advice, or your assistance, sir. She is not happy at Mr. Mellish's. People come there she does not like."

"Is Mr. Skipworth still there?"

"He is, sir. And there are a number of other gentlemen who come and go. They are all very polite to Monsieur de Severac and his daughter, but Mademoiselle Jeanne, I think, does not feel at ease with them."

"She wants to leave Bellevue and come with her father here to Philadelphia?"

"That might be her desire, Mr. Lee. She was very eager to have you get her message, and without the knowledge of any one but myself." Sebastien shook his gray head. "I am very much to blame for losing her letter."

"Sebastien," said Jared, "the first time you drove Mademoiselle Jeanne here I was sitting at the window and I saw a man in a brown coat come around the corner opposite and stare at her as if he had seen her before. I saw you catch sight of him and shake your fist at him, and then he slunk away. You remember that?"

"Indeed I do, Mr. Lee. But I didn't know any one saw him but myself."

"He's an enemy of your master and his daughter?"

"He's a villain, sir. I never want to see him again."

"I saw him that same night in the woods near Bellevue; he knows where the Marquis is. You didn't see him today at the inn or around the stables?"

Sebastien shook his head. "I did not, sir. I've only seen him the one time you mention, that day here in the city."

"All right. I didn't speak to the Marquis or Mademoiselle Jeanne about him because I knew you'd seen him and knew who he was."

"He's a rascal, sir, but I can't think he'd do them any harm here in this new country."

Jared wasn't so sure about that, but now his immediate concern was to find out the contents of the missing letter and learn how he could aid Jeanne. "I think somebody stole that letter," he said, "and, if that is so, I must learn what was in it."

"I have been very stupid, Mr. Lee, very much to blame."

The old retainer—whom Jared knew to have been a wonderfully faithful servant to his master during those trying days in France—looked so utterly disconsolate and self-condemning that Jared took pity on him. "Any man might have met with the same mischance, Sebastien," he said kindly. "And since you haven't Mademoiselle Jeanne's letter for me, the simplest plan is for me to ride to Bellevue with you and speak to her myself."

"Will you do that, Mr. Lee?" asked Sebastien eagerly.

"I will; and at once." Jared went to Mr. Carroll's

writing-table, penned a few words, and placed the note where the lawyer would be certain to find it. "Now you come with me while I get my mare, and we'll remedy the lost letter before sunset."

It took but a few minutes to have the roan saddled, and then Jared and Sebastien set out for the lower ferry. In his coat Jared had a new pistol he had bought since losing his first one to the highwayman; if he returned after dark he might want it. It occurred to him that possibly he would spend the night at the Green Anchor, question Oakes and the hostler regarding the men who had talked with Sebastien, and ride back to town next morning.

The ferry crossed, they rode south, Sebastien for the most part silent, Jared's thoughts busy with speculation as to what Jeanne wanted of him. The secrecy that she had enjoined on Sebastien indicated that she mistrusted those at Mellish's house.

The thought of this presently led Jared to say to his companion, "Mademoiselle Jeanne would probably prefer that I talk with her in private, that I shouldn't ride up to the house where Mr. Mellish or Mr. Skipworth or others would see me. I will go on to the Green Anchor Inn, making up some story about Mr. Carroll's having sent me there on business, and you shall see your mistress and bring me word what she wishes me to do."

"That would be the best plan, Mr. Lee," Sebastien agreed.

"If she wants to talk with me in secret I could take the path along the river after dark and meet her at the grove at the foot of Mr. Mellish's lawn. Doubtless she could invent some reason for going outdoors alone, and you could come with her, Sebastien." After a moment Jared added, "Yes, I want to see her; I prefer that to her sending another message. We will arrange it this way. If for any reason she cannot meet me on the river path in front of Bellevue after dark you will bring me word at the inn, otherwise I will go there and expect to see her. And now you ride on ahead. It's best we shouldn't be seen together coming to the inn."

Sebastien trotted on, to return his hired mount to the hostler and proceed on foot to Mellish's. Allowing him time to do this, Jared rode into the stable yard, sprang down, turned the roan over to the boy, and went into the tavern. He made up a plausible story about having had to see a farmer in the neighborhood on legal business of Mr. Carroll's, which he told Simeon Oakes, and ordered an early supper. While this was preparing he strolled out to the stable in search of information. The hostler was not there, however, and the boy in charge could give him no information about any men who had been there since noon.

There were no other guests at the inn, and Jared ate his supper by himself, his thoughts centring on his coming meeting with Jeanne. What was it she wanted to tell him? What help was it she required? In any event he meant to befriend her to the utmost of his power.

Twilight drew on. If Jeanne, for any reason, could not arrange to meet him on the river bank, she would by now have sent him word by Sebastien. There had been plenty of time for Sebastien to come with a message. So, as it grew dark, and the candles of night were lighted in the dark blue bowl of the sky, Jared left the inn and walked down to the Delaware.

He took the path north along the river, meeting no one, absent-mindedly noting the few boats that floated indistinctly on the dim surface of the stream. Winding in and out through low bushes and clumps of willow and alder he followed the road that led by a gradual ascent toward the promontory of Bellevue. He heard the night call of a homing bird in a thicket on his left. At the moment he was wondering what excuse Jeanne would use to slip away from the house and come down to the river to meet him. Would she rouse Skipworth's suspicions? Skipworth was a man who suspected everyone.

Just beyond the thicket a sapling, uprooted, lay across the path. Jared stooped to lift it and throw it out of the way. As he bent over something struck him sharply behind the left ear. He staggered and saw stars. Then another blow caught him squarely on the head, and he went down, crashing into the tree.

XI

ADVENTURE ON THE WATER

JARED, opening his eyes, saw the night sky far above him and heard the gurgle of water against the side of a moving boat. His head ached terrifically, however, and he felt faint and dizzy, so he shut his eyes and lay motionless, not caring where he was.

After a time he felt himself lifted up, and was aware half-consciously that he was being handed over the gunwale of a boat. He saw dim moving figures and stationary objects and heard a murmur of voices. He was being carried somewhere, but he felt little interest in his destination. Something hot and tingling was being poured down his throat. He was lying on something soft and comfortable. He moved his head to see where he was, but this brought back the ache in his temples, and he shut his eyes again and kept still.

When he awoke he felt stiff and sore, and lay for some time trying to get his bearings. He was in a ship's bunk; daylight coming in at a porthole above him showed a small cabin, with a single door. There was no sound outside, and the vessel did not seem to be moving. Very gingerly he put his fingers to his forehead and found that it was band-

146

HE WAS AWARE HALF-CONSCIOUSLY THAT HE WAS BEING HANDED OVER
THE GUNWALE OF A BOAT

aged.   He thought that at one place, where the bandage hurt when he touched it, it was caked with blood.   He wet his lips, which were dry, with his tongue, and took an easier position.

He began to remember now.   He had been going to meet Jeanne de Severac at the grove in front of Mr. Mellish's when he had stooped over an uprooted sapling on the path along the river and something had struck him on the head.   Some enemy had waylaid him and brought him out to this boat.   He could not imagine who his enemy could be; why any one should think it worth while to treat him in such fashion; but nevertheless here he was in a cabin on a strange ship.

He was very thirsty and was wondering whether he should get up and go in search of something to drink when he heard sounds outside the porthole. Easing himself to a sitting posture he looked through the small, round window and saw a man on the deck below him.   This man was speaking to someone over the side of the ship.   A moment later this second man appeared, climbing over the rail as if from a small boat moored alongside.   He jumped down to the deck, and immediately put his hand into his coat pocket.   Withdrawing it he held up a small object, as though for the inspection of the first man.

Jared was directly above them, and he saw that the object looked like a round gold coin, with four deep notches cut in it, one at each quarter of the circle. It appeared to have some special significance, for the first man, seeing it, nodded, and touched his finger to his head. Then the two walked forward, talking, and were lost to Jared's sight.

He sat there for some time, wondering and looking through the porthole. The boat on which he was stood well out from shore. He did not recognize the bank of the river at this point; it was low and marshy with no houses in sight. Everything was quiet, no ships were passing, no fishing boats were moving along the green shore.

Presently he got up from the bunk and walking over to the door quietly tried the latch. The door was, as he suspected, fastened on the outside. Someone had made him a prisoner; someone had taken the pistol from his coat. He glanced about the cabin; there was only a rude chest of drawers, a three-legged stool, a row of wooden pegs on which hung an assortment of old clothes. His head was commencing to throb again, so he sat down on the bunk.

An interval, and there was the sound of footfalls outside the cabin. Someone lifted the latch and the door was opened inward. The man whom Jared had seen when he first looked through the porthole came into the room with a nod and a smile.

"That's better," said the man. "I thought you'd

feel as right as a trivet this morning. You've a hard head, my lad."

Jared was agreeably disappointed. This fellow was no ogre; he was tall and broad, with a crop of red hair and a sunburnt, lively face.

"I'd like a drink," said Jared.

"Aye, so you would. I'll fetch you one in a minute."

The man went out, and almost immediately returned with a water bottle and a tin cup. He filled the cup and handed it to Jared, who gulped the water down and asked for more. The second cup drained, Jared felt much better. "What's the meaning of this?" he said. "Who brought me out here?"

The man placed the bottle and cup on the chest of drawers and sat down on the three-legged stool. "You might as well keep such questions to yourself," he said, "they're a waste of breath. How's your head this morning?"

"I want to know who I've got to thank for that bump and this bandage."

"You can thank me for the bandage. I'll take it off and put on a fresh one by and by. In a day or two you won't know anything struck you. What might be your name?"

Jared hesitated, but could see no reason for secrecy on his part. "Jared Lee. I live in Philadelphia, and I've friends there who will want to know what's become of me."

"No doubt they will, Jared. Well, let them ask. Questions don't hurt no one. My name's Bill Kitt. Just you take things easy. Breakfast will be ready pretty soon."

"If you were in my place I don't believe you'd take things so easy!" Jared retorted warmly.

"Oh, yes I would," said Kitt. "Nice day for a sail down the river and nothing to do but enjoy yourself. Pretty prime I call it, if you ask me."

There was no advantage in remonstrance; argument only made his head throb. Moreover the odor of cooking that was now coming in at the open door was quite enticing. Jared smiled.

"That's right, my lad," said Kitt. "I've got no grudge against you. I put you in my bunk last night and I bound up your head. Couldn't ask no fairer than that, could you? All you've got to do is mind what I say, and there'll be no bones broken." He accompanied this last with a broad grin; then added, "Now you stay where you are, and I'll fetch you some breakfast."

Shortly he brought in a battered tin tray, and Jared found his appetite sufficient to dispose of a cup of coffee, several slices of sizzling bacon and some bread. Then Kitt placed a pitcher of water and a basin on the chest, and Jared washed him-

self. Afterwards Kitt removed the caked bandage
from Jared's head and bound a fresh one over
his bruises.

The boat was now moving south on the Delaware.
Jared judged the craft to be a small one, with only
a few men in her crew, and Kitt her commander.
The latter, when he had finished the new bandage,
left the cabin, securing the door on the outside,
and Jared whiled away the time looking through
the porthole.

He saw marshlands and meadows, strips of woods,
occasional villages and many solitary farmsteads;
nearer, on the river, ships of various rigs and sizes
passed before his eyes. He saw men on the decks,
but they were too far off to hail, and even if they
should hear his voice they were hardly likely to
pay it any attention. He was a prisoner, and for
the present it seemed he must remain so.

He sought for a reason to explain why he was
a captive in this man Kitt's cabin. It might be—
it must be—it seemed to him, because he had come
to the Green Anchor Inn on business concerning
Jeanne. Someone had known of his presence there,
and wanted him out of the way.

Mr. Carroll would know from the note Jared
had left on his table that he had ridden to the Green
Anchor with Sebastien, and after a day or two
might send to the inn to learn what had become of

his student; but Oakes would not know nor would Sebastien or Jeanne, and by that time Jared might be anywhere, possibly sailing out on the Atlantic Ocean.

Jared judged it must be about noon when Kitt reappeared, this time bringing a bowl in which was a steaming stew of meat mixed with onions and carrots. Kitt did not wait while Jared ate, but returned for the empty bowl later. He proffered no information, and Jared asked for none, knowing well that questions would be idle.

Mid of the afternoon the boat turned shoreward, and, having come to the mouth of a small creek, anchored off the bank. Jared saw open fields and at a distance of a quarter-mile a white house and a barn. There the boat rested, while Jared, caged in the cabin, grew more and more impatient. He thought of many things he wanted to say.

It was not until after dusk, however, that Kitt again opened the door. "You're going ashore with me," he said brusquely, "and mind you play no tricks. So long as you do what you're told there'll be no trouble, but if you don't I've a pistol here, and I'll use it."

"What is this place?" asked Jared.

Kitt shook his finger at the questioner. "Now drop that, do you understand? You're not to ask questions. You won't find everyone as civil to you

as I be. Just you come along and do as you're
told. You don't look like a fool and I hope you
won't act like one." He nodded toward the door.
"Step out on deck."

Jared, with Kitt at his elbow, left the cabin and
came out on deck. A couple of men, who were
lounging at the rail, turned to eye him. "Follow
me into the small boat," said Kitt, swinging over
the side.

Jared dropped down on to a thwart. Kitt picked
up a pair of oars, and in a few minutes had rowed
to a float, where another small boat was tied. "Get
out," commanded Kitt; and Jared stepped to the
float. He had decided that the best thing for him
to do was to obey orders.

They went up by a footpath between two plowed
fields, and so to the white house with the barn on
its left. A light shone in a window and a small
spiral of smoke rose from a chimney. Kitt knocked
on the front door, and, after a brief interval, it
was opened. A young woman in a brown linen dress
looked out at them.

"Here's your boarder, Rachel," said Kitt; "Jared
Lee, from Philadelphia."

It seemed that Jared was expected. The young
woman, who was pretty, made a curtsy, to which
Jared responded with a bow. "Come in," she invited. "I was just setting supper on the table. I

know you're hungry, Bill; you always are, you big bear."

At a prod from Kitt's elbow Jared stepped indoors. He was in the main room of the house, kitchen and dining-room combined. At one end was a great fireplace, with a back-bar of iron curving along the brick top, from which a number of pots and kettles were suspended by chains. A back-log was blazing and throwing a ruddy glow into the room, which was also lighted by a couple of candles in pewter holders that stood on the supper table some distance from the hearth. A gray-haired woman was cutting bread at the table, and a tall, long-limbed man was lounging in an arm-chair, one leg swung over the other.

"Fetched him, did you, Bill?" said the man, looking at Jared.

"Here he is," answered Kitt. "Pa and Ma Powell, Jared Lee, from Philadelphia."

Again Jared, feeling it was best to appear civil, made a bow, though the man in the chair only gave him a cursory nod and the woman, after one incurious glance at him, continued slicing bread.

"He can give you all the news from Philadelphia, Rachel," Kitt went on. "He'll tell you what the gals are wearing."

"I know that myself, thank you, Bill," retorted the young woman, tossing her head. "Just because we live down here in Delaware, we're not so much behind the times."

Kitt laughed, and with easy familiarity put his arm around Rachel's waist. "You're not anyhow, Rachel. There's not a prettier gal between Chester and the Capes."

"Mind your manners, you big bear! Don't you see we've got company?" With a push Rachel slipped out of Kitt's grasp.

"Jared's not company," said Kitt. "I don't mind his knowing that Rachel Powell's my gal."

While this talk went on Jared wondered why Kitt had brought him to the farmhouse. It was clear that Farmer Powell and his wife, as well as Rachel, had been expecting him, therefore Kitt must have sent word to them or been to see them before he fetched Jared ashore.

Kitt's last remark served to direct Rachel's attention again to the young stranger who stood, embarrassed, in the centre of the kitchen. "Did Bill bandage your head?" she asked. "Does it hurt now?"

"Not very much," Jared answered.

"I bandaged it," Kitt asserted. "You might put on a fresh one after supper, Rachel. It's not his head, but his stomach, that needs tending now."

On that hint the young woman bustled about with her preparations for the meal, assisted by Kitt, who at her direction brought plates, cups, forks and knives from a dresser and set them out on the table. Jared sat down on a bench and watched the proceedings. Farmer Powell, morose and silent, appeared lost in his own reflections.

When supper was ready they all drew up to the table. There was a soup, flavored with leeks, into which bread was crumbled, a big meat pie, which contained a variety of vegetables, and a baked Indian meal pudding. Rachel served the men with ale. Kitt and Powell ate greedily, like men who had worked hard outdoors all day; Mrs. Powell was sparing with her spoon and fork; her daughter took a bite now and then, when she was not busy refilling the plates of the men.

The table was cleared by the two women. Farmer Powell, drawing his chair closer to the fireplace, produced a cake of tobacco, from which, with a knife, he chipped small slices into the bowl of his pipe. Kitt also filled a pipe, and lighted it from a sliver on the hearth. "Well now, Jared," he said, "you can't complain of your situation, can you?"

"I'd like to know why I'm here," answered Jared, who had taken a chair near the two men.

"He's the greatest hand at asking questions," Kitt observed, looking at Powell.

The farmer hunched his shoulders. "I don't know anything about it," he grunted.

"Nor do I," said Kitt. "I only know them's my

orders. Jared's to stay where he is. Maybe, after a day or two, they'll be sending him on a voyage to the Indies."

"Somebody's going to pay for this!" muttered Jared, stung by Kitt's joking manner.

"Might make a sailor out of you," Kitt continued. He pulled at his pipe for a moment. "Be you connected with any of the shipping merchants in the city?"

"No," said Jared. "I'm studying law with Mr. Nathaniel Carroll."

"Huh; that's not it, then. But there's some proper reason for keeping you close. 'Tain't my business, and in a manner of speaking it don't seem to be yours either."

Rachel presently joined them, and now she unwound the bandage about Jared's head. She brought a basin of warm water and washed his wound, where the blood had caked. Then, with a strip of fresh linen, she rebound his head. Her fingers were deft and gentle. Jared thanked her and she smiled at him.

"There now, Mr. Jared, you're not frightened of us, are you?"

"Not in the least."

"I know Bill's a terrible fellow; but this isn't his house."

"Hold on there, Rachel," put in Kitt. "Don't you put wrong notions into his head. You're all to do as I tell you here, and that's to see that Jared don't leave this house."

"He won't, Bill, you big bear."

"That's right; he won't," said Kitt positively. "There'll be a man from the boat watching his window all night."

"He wouldn't try to leave, Bill. Pa sleeps in the next room, and he's got a gun."

Powell nodded, his eyes frowning at Jared from under his shaggy brows, and shambled off upstairs. His wife had already disappeared, presumably to her chamber. After a few minutes Kitt stood up. "We'll show Jared to his room now, Rachel. Time he was getting to bed."

The young woman took a candle and led Jared and Kitt up the stairs. She opened the door of a small room at the front of the house, went in and lighted a candle that stood on a bureau.

"Cosy I call this," said Kitt. "Go along downstairs, Rachel. I'll be down in a minute."

Rachel went out, and Kitt turned to Jared. "Here you are, and here you'll stay for the present. I meant what I said. There'll be a man on guard outside this window, and his orders are to shoot. If you know what's wise for you, you'll keep right here. Pa Powell wouldn't think no more of potting you than he would of potting a rabbit."

With these pleasant words Kitt departed. Jared

heard the key turn in the lock of his door. He had no thought of trying to escape; he knew that Kitt, for all his light manner, meant what he said.

He opened the window and looked out.   The fields were silver in the moon.   Beyond them he saw the mast of the ship, pointing upward like a finger, and beyond that the river, a broad expanse with no opposite shoreline visible.

This place must be near to Lewes, near the Delaware Capes, not far from the open sea.

He took off some of his clothes and lay down on the bed. After a time he heard voices outside the house, and, rising, tiptoed to the window. Below stood three men, one of whom he recognized as Kitt. He could not hear what they said, though he listened intently, for he felt sure they were discussing him. Presently one of them moved away toward the river, another sat down on the door-step, and Kitt went round the house.

Jared got into bed again.   Any attempt he might make to escape must be postponed to the morrow.

XII

TWO FIGHTING MEN

THE sound of heavy boots clumping about in the room next door woke Jared in the morning. Farmer Powell was probably rising early to attend to his stock. A rooster somewhere sent forth his lusty and exultant cock-a-doodle-do. Jared rubbed his eyes and smiled. He had heard such a greeting of the dawn from the barnyard almost every morning at his Lancaster home.

The heavy boots went clumping down the stairs, and Jared fell to wondering at the strange chance that had made him, a law-abiding and respectable young fellow, a prisoner at this farmhouse near the mouth of the Delaware. The Powells themselves certainly had no grudge against him, they were probably being paid to give him a room and food for as long a time as Kitt should be directed to keep him there. Possibly Kitt had himself suggested this particular farmhouse, for the red-haired man was clearly very fond of the pretty Rachel.

Jared rose, and, finding a pitcher of water, a basin and a towel on a stand, washed his face and hands. The bandage on his head was stiff, but otherwise his hurts gave him little discomfort. As

160

he dressed he looked out the window; the sun, now risen some distance above the river, was warming the fields. There were no houses to be seen; beyond the farm was an expanse of fruit trees, a sea of pink and white. The boat, that had lain off the mouth of the creek, was no longer there.

Rachel's voice spoke outside the door. "Are you up?"

"Aye," answered Jared.

A key turned in the lock. "Breakfast is ready."

Jared opened the door and followed the young woman down the steep, narrow stairs. In the kitchen was the appetizing odor of frying ham and boiling coffee.

Mrs. Powell, a small, gray figure, looked up from her seat at the table and gave him a nod and a "Good-morning." Rachel poured him a cup of coffee and put a slice of ham and bread and butter on his plate. The farmer had had his breakfast and was not in the room; neither was Bill Kitt, though a clean plate and tumbler indicated to Jared that the man was expected.

Rachel, looking very fresh and blooming, had a smile for Jared as she sat opposite him at table. "Sleep well?" she inquired.

"Like a log."

"I told Bill you wouldn't be stirring about. Tell me, what are the ladies wearing in Philadelphia?"

Jared considered a moment. "Why, light, summery dresses—what they always wear in spring."

Rachel laughed, and was about to ask another question when the front door opened and Kitt came in.

"Aha, breakfast!" he exclaimed. "And here's Jared, none the worse for a good night's sleep, I'll be bound! Good-morning, Ma Powell." He spoke in a loud voice to the older woman, who was deaf, and went round to Rachel and gave her a hearty kiss.

"Bill, you big bear!" said Rachel, pretending to push him away. "What will he think?" And she pointed her fork at Jared.

"He'll think that we're going to be married, and very soon. And he'll think right. That's why I brought you down here, Jared," he added; "to show you what a lucky fellow I be." He drew up a chair to the table, and, sitting down, helped himself to ham and coffee. "We're only waiting till my ship comes in, and there's so many sailing now it oughtn't to be long till I get one. I'm not partic'lar about her cargo, rum or slaves or anything that'll fetch gold. Rachel here sets a great store on gowns."

"Don't talk that way, Bill," admonished Rachel. "Mr. Jared might misunderstand you."

Kitt glanced at Jared. "Maybe he might, and then again maybe he mightn't. But I don't think he'll tell any one."

After breakfast Kitt said to Jared, "You're free of the house, but not free beyond it. By night the boat'll be back, and I'll know what to do with you. Meantime make yourself easy, but remember I've got an eye on you."

Kitt was, it appeared, a jack of all trades, and he busied himself with doing a score of chores about the farmhouse. There was a chair to be mended, a shelf to be put up, a candle-mould to be soldered. He went from the house to the barn, he worked outside the front door, he hammered and sawed the while he hummed snatches of song; but Jared knew that if he made any move to escape Kitt would instantly stop him.

"Want to make me a broom?" Rachel asked Jared. "There's a pile of hemlock branches in the shed. Bill will fetch them for you, and I'll give you a jack-knife and some hempen twine."

Jared had often made hemlock brooms at his own home, and he much preferred any occupation to idleness. So Kitt brought the branches and Jared, sitting on the doorstep, trimmed them to the proper length and shape, tied them and wound them with twine and fitted them into a long handle, which he rounded and smoothed with a knife. The broom completed, he turned his attention to whittling some clothespins for Rachel, and by the time he had

turned out a half-dozen of these Farmer Powell
came in and the family sat down to dinner.

After dinner the farmer returned to his plowing
in a distant field at the rear of the house, his wife
went to her room, Rachel sat down with her knitting.
Kitt lighted his pipe and seated himself by Jared on
the doorstep, keeping up a light chatter with his
sweetheart over his shoulder.

The warm sun and the hearty dinner made Jared
drowsy. He leaned his head against the doorpost
and half-shut his eyes. Presently he saw a man
coming up the road toward the house. There was
something familiar about the figure, and as the
man drew near he saw it was Luke Hatch.

Kitt was busily talking, but as Hatch stopped in
the road before the farmhouse he broke off his conversation with Rachel and eyed the stranger. "What
do you want here?" he said truculently.

"I want a boat," answered Hatch. "I want to
row down to Lewes."

"We haven't got a boat for you."

"They told me up the road I'd find a boat in the
creek. I'll pay you for it."

"No, you won't," declared Kitt. "There's no
boat in the creek for a stranger."

All this time Hatch, though he couldn't but have
seen Jared sitting on the doorstep, had given no

sign that he recognized him. Now he stepped nearer, his face flushing at Kitt's surly words and manner.

"Do you own the boat?" he asked. "You talk as if you owned the whole creation."

"Speak him gently, Bill," whispered Rachel, leaning forward.

"Never you mind who owns it," Kitt threw back. "I've got the say in this part of the country."

"Oh, you have?" jeered Hatch. "Well, now, let me tell you; you keep a civil tongue in your head when you're speaking to me!"

Kitt got to his feet and pointed his pipe at the stocky man who was glowering at him. "You be on your way! You're not wanted 'round here!"

Hatch spat on one broad hand and rubbed it on the other. "You're not the man to send me," he said in a level voice.

"Oh, Bill—" murmured Rachel.

Disregarding her, Kitt, his face now red with anger, stepped out on the grass. "I could put a bullet through you," he said, reaching under his coat.

To Jared's great surprise, however, Luke Hatch was ready for him. From underneath his butternut coat he drew a pistol. "If that's what you want —" he retorted. "But seeing there's a woman present, I'd rather we didn't use lead."

"Oh, stop, Bill! Stop, for my sake!" begged Rachel, now standing beside Kitt.

"That's right, Mistress," said Hatch. "Fists were made for fighting." He looked at Kitt with a taunting grin which twisted the scar on his cheek. "I've fought better men than you with my fists. Want to try a go at it?"

"I can knock you into a pudding!" Kitt declared loudly.

Hatch made a face that with his crooked nose and his scarred cheek gave him a devilish leer. "Ah now, that's talking! That's what I like to hear! If you knock me into a pudding you can crow so loud about it they'll hear you over in Spain. See here, my bully bantam; I'll put my coat, with my pistol in the pocket, twenty paces off to the east if you'll put yours, with your pistol, as far to the west. And the lad who's sitting on the doorstep can see to fair play."

This last remark served to remind Kitt of Jared's presence, for indeed in his desire to outface this free-spoken fellow and send him about his business he had forgotten for the moment his obligation to guard his prisoner. "Hm—m," he temporized. "I can knock that ugly head of yours off your shoulders; but there's something to be seen to first. If you want a fight, stay where you are, and I'll be with you in a minute. If you don't, get along with you, and take your braggart words somewhere else."

"I'll stay," said Hatch. "I never ran away from a fight yet."

All this time Rachel had been clutching Kitt's arm, muttering to him. Now Kitt swept her in at the door. "Get into the house!" he ordered Jared, catching the young fellow by the coat.

"Rachel, that hempen twine," Kitt continued when they were in the kitchen. He seized a chair and as Rachel quickly brought the twine and a jack-knife he ordered Jared to sit down. This command he emphasized by the sight of a pistol. Jared sat down, and Kitt in a moment had his prisoner's hands bound at the wrists and his elbows made fast to the chair.

"There," grunted Kitt, "that'll hold you. Rachel, you stay here, while I teach that braggart his manners."

"But, Bill—" she began.

"You can shut the door and bolt it, if you've a mind to," he broke in.

With that he was out of the house again, and on the stretch of grass beside the road where Hatch stood waiting.

Rachel didn't shut the door. She stood with her hands clasped, watching the two men outside.

"Twenty paces," said Hatch. Jared saw Kitt nod, and turn on his heel. Each man stripped off his coat and laid it on the ground. They walked back, rolling up their sleeves and spitting on their hands.

Kitt was the taller fellow, but in brawn they seemed evenly matched. For a moment or two they danced about, limbering their muscles, then suddenly Kitt drove his right fist out, aimed at Hatch's chin.

Hatch ducked, and the blow fell harmless. An uppercut landed on Kitt's cheek. Jared caught a low cry from Rachel, whose hand was on the back of his chair.

The men were mixing it now, circling round and round, knees crooked, heads up, down, sideways, filled with the lust of battle.

There was in-fighting. Hatch's nose was bleeding. They broke away, glared at each other, came back again like bulls.

An even match for five minutes. Then Kitt landed a blow on Hatch's cheek that sent the man staggering. Kitt followed it up. Hatch gave ground, warding off the tempest. Now Hatch straightened up and caught Kitt in the right eye, blackening that orb and making Kitt rock on his feet.

A battle of giants, for they were tough and hardy, and each had fought many fights. But presently it was Kitt who gave ground and who warded more often than struck. A lull, a moment's respite; Kitt, springing forward, drove a terrific left. Hatch bent, and as his enemy's fist ripped along his ear he sent in a righthander to the point of the chin.

Kitt went down, knocked out clean, legs doubled up.

Hatch bent over him, hands on his knees, catching his breath.

There was a cry from the woman in the kitchen and she ran through the doorway.

"No bones broken, my girl," said Hatch. "Your man's a rare fighter. The wind's knocked out of him, that's all. He'll be around in a minute."

Rachel dropped to her knees beside Kitt.

"Water; that's what he wants, a dash of cold water," Hatch recommended. "I'll get a bucket and fill it at the well."

Rachel paid no attention to him, she was murmuring to Kitt.

"A bucket," repeated Hatch, and turned to the door of the farmhouse.

He ran into the kitchen, and his eyes lighted on Jared. "I knew it was you, sir," he said in a whisper. "I've a knife in my breeches."

In a twinkling he had the doubled thongs of hempen twine cut loose. "Now, sir, when I bring that fellow in at the door you get out by a window. Make for the boat in the creek as fast as you can run. But stop long enough on the way to pick up his pistol."

Jared sprang to a window beyond the door, which would shield him from any one entering.

Hatch snatched up a bucket from the hearth and went outdoors. "What do you say?" He was addressing Rachel. "Shall I get him into the house before I fetch the water?"

"Don't you touch him!" stormed the young woman. "Get out of my sight!"

"In a minute, in a minute," Hatch answered soothingly. "I won't hurt him. I swear I admire him. He's a fighter to my own taste. See." He pushed her gently away and put his arms under Kitt. Then bending his broad back, he half-lifted and half-dragged the inert Kitt to the door.

Rachel came after him, and as Hatch raised his burden over the doorstep Jared opened a window. The next moment he had dropped over the sill and stood outside on the grass.

He ran to Kitt's coat, picked it up, felt for the inside pocket and the pistol. The coat was upside down and the pistol slipped out, and with it something else, a round piece of gold metal cut with four notches. Jared snatched pistol and gold piece, and took to his legs, running by the footpath between the plowed fields to the float in the creek.

The rowboat he had seen on the evening before was still there and he stepped aboard and sat down. He looked at the disk of gold; it bore a king's head and a French inscription. It was probably a French coin. But the notches, like the four points of a compass cut in its circumference, indicated that it had now another significance. He remembered where he had seen such a token before, the man who had come aboard the ship on the river had shown such a coin to Kitt.

There was a shout on the footpath, and Hatch, his coat on his arm, came leaping down to the float. Jared stuck the gold piece into his pocket.

"There's a mighty racket back there!" exclaimed Hatch. "The young woman and an old dame, who came downstairs, shouting their heads off, and my lusty fighting man sitting up and swearing. But I've got you away, and that's what I came for! Two pair of oars; we'll be out of sight long before they set the dogs on!"

Propelled by two rowers, the boat shot along the creek and came out into the river. Upstream it turned, and soon was a good mile above the farmstead.

"Easy now, sir," said Hatch. "All we've got to do is paddle along in comfort." He drew in his oars, resting them on the gunwales. "Yon man was a rare fighter. He's got a mighty punch, but he lacks the science. With a little teaching he'd make a good 'un." Hatch chuckled. "'Twas luck he didn't know who I be. But maybe he'd have fought regardless. I could see he was spoiling for a mill;

red head, that's the kind, sir; you can bait 'em every time."

"Did you know I was there," asked Jared, "before you came to the house?"

"No, sir, I wasn't certain till I saw you sitting in the door. Happened this way: I was at the Green Anchor night before last and I heard from Oakes you'd been there; 'Mr. Lee,' he said, 'the young gentleman from Philadelphia you was talking with a week or so ago.' Your horse was in the stable, so I knew you must be somewhere about; and I thought I'd look alongshore. Well, sir, I went by the path, and I saw a couple of men carrying someone down to a skiff. That set me to thinking, and I followed, keeping out of their sight. I made out as how it might be you they had, and I caught a glimpse of one of the men, and recognized him as Bill Kitt. Kitt don't know me, but I've seen him before, and I've heard he had a girl, one o' the Powells down Lewes way. So, thinks I, maybe I can find out what this Kitt is up to, and what's happened to Mr. Lee if I look up the wench at Powell's. I didn't think that all out at once; it came to me next morning. What did they want of you, sir?"

"I don't know any more than you do," answered Jared. "But, Mr. Hatch, I owe you a thousand thanks. You've done me a rare good turn."

"Call me Luke, it sounds more nat'ral. Well, you see, I couldn't sleep easy at nights thinkin' maybe they was going to misuse you. No, sir, that I couldn't. The bloody pirates!"

"I'm going to find out what's at the bottom of all this," said Jared. "There's a law for criminals."

"Aye, there's a law," agreed Hatch, though in a doubtful tone. "There's a law in the city, but there ain't so much of a law along this river. Time for another spell of rowing, Mr. Lee. The further we get away from Lewes the better."

XIII

JARED ASKS QUESTIONS

A COUPLE of miles above the creek Hatch and Jared ran their rowboat on to a sandy beach, got out, and pulled the boat to dry land. Then Hatch led the way across the river meadows to the nearest road and soon pointed out a farmhouse. "I left my market-cart with the man here," he said, "and footed it on to Powell's. Farmer Fishburn's an old friend of mine. I come down in the fall and go gunning with him."

The farmer was at work in a field and Hatch called a greeting to him. In the barn was the horse and the cart, and speedily Jared and his friend were bumping over the rough country road northward. Now Jared related his adventures in detail and Hatch listened and rubbed his chin and put in a word now and then. But he found no answer to the riddle Jared propounded, and they were still mulling over it when, having jogged through a number of sleepy, straggling villages and over many miles of rutted road, they came, an hour after sunset, to the vicinity of the Green Anchor Inn.

"Your horse will be still in the stable," said Hatch. "Will you stop for supper here?"

174

"I don't want to go into the tavern," said Jared, "but I must get my mare."

Hatch nodded understandingly. "That might be best," he agreed. "I could give you a bite at my house, and a bed for the night, if 't would be of service to you."

"It would," said Jared, "for there's some business here I must see to as soon as I can. There's a French lady, a Mademoiselle de Severac, who is staying at Mr. Mellish's house, and I want a word with her." He looked at his companion. "I'm already ever so much in your debt, Luke; but I'm going to ask if you'll do me another favor. I don't want to go up to Mellish's, but I must see the French lady."

"Aye," said Hatch, smiling. "And what would you have me do?"

"Get a message to her, if you can. She and her father have a servant named Sebastien. Will you see if you can find him at Mellish's? And if you can speak with him alone, ask him to tell his mistress that Jared Lee will be waiting in the road to Bellevue, a little way this side of the house, wanting a word with her? When you've given that message, wait for me in the highroad. I'll get my mare and come on at once."

"Sebastien? Aye, I've seen him at the tavern. I'll make up some tale to tell him if there's any one about, and when I have him to myself I'll slip your word to him."

Jared jumped from the cart, and Hatch, clucking to his weary horse, drove on.

Jared was hatless, and his head was bandaged, a figure calculated to raise questions; but fortunately the only person in the stableyard was the boy, and he knew better than to put his curiosity in words. There was still money in Jared's pocket and he gave a coin to the boy, helped saddle the mare, and rode out without interruption.

A whip-poor-will sang in the woods as he drew rein near the head of the road to Bellevue. Beyond he could see in the starlight Hatch's empty cart, the patient horse nibbling a young maple. Jared dismounted, and leading his mare into the low bushes, tied her to a tree. He waited ten, twenty minutes before he heard feet on the drive.

It was Hatch. "I found your man," he said. "He promised to give the lady your message. I'll watch your horse, Mr. Lee, and if you need any help you call out. You've got Bill Kitt's pistol?"

Jared nodded. "You're a true friend, Luke." Then he turned into the road to the east and silently, with eyes and ears alert, went up between the dark trees.

When he saw open lawn before him he stopped and drew aside in the woods. The night was very quiet. Away back of him the whip-poor-will at intervals sounded his ghostly note. A twig crackled now and again under the foot of some small nocturnal-hunting creature. Jared began to think that Jeanne had found it impossible to leave the house. And then he saw a cloaked figure, a girl's figure, crossing the lawn and coming toward the trees.

She was alone, and he stepped out. As she drew near he murmured, "It's I, Mademoiselle, Jared Lee."

She came close, without a word. Then she put her hand on his arm. "What happened to you two nights ago? I went to the path by the river. Oh, you're hurt! Your head is bandaged!"

He drew her into the underbrush, away from the road where some starlight fell between the branches. "I'm all right now. I was knocked on the head and shipped down the river. I don't know why. But what can I do to serve you?"

"I sent Sebastien to you," she explained, "because I could think of no one else who might be able to help us. Jacques Latour is here! I was walking by the river three days ago, and I saw him in a small boat. He didn't see me; but it was Jacques Latour. What is he doing here?"

Latour! That must be the man in brown! thought Jared. "Who is he?" he asked.

"The man who led the mob when they came to our château, the man who planned our ruin!"

It was so dark where they stood in the woods that he could not see her face distinctly, but he knew by the thrill in her voice how much she was affected by the arrival of this Frenchman. "Why should he have come across the ocean," he asked, "when he and villains like him are having their own way in France?"

"I don't know. He's not a simple peasant. His father is a notary in our village in Normandy, and Jacques, from what I've heard of him, has been a leader in the Jacobin Club. Can it be that he hates my father—who always dealt kindly with the people —so much that he has followed him here with some evil plan in his mind?"

"There was a man who saw you drive up to Mr. Carroll's; I've spoken with him; he talks like a foreigner. But you have friends. This isn't France, Mademoiselle; he can't harm you here."

"Can he not? Oh, Master Jared, think of your own experience! Ever since that night when they came to our house with arms and torches, like so many wild beasts, I have put no limit to what mad men may do! They are hunting us down like wolves in France, like wolves crazed with hunger. And if one of those mad men were to follow us here—" She broke off, her breath coming quickly. Then she added more quietly, "As for friends, I put little trust in those about us at Bellevue."

"Mr. Mellish means you well surely?"

There was a brief hesitation. "Perhaps he does. I think he likes entertaining my father, for some notion that his presence here gives distinction to his house. But Mr. Mellish is not a man to inspire my confidence."

"Well," said Jared, "Mr. Mellish isn't a man I should rely on myself. Nor his friend, Skipworth. No, you must leave Bellevue, and come to Philadelphia. Mr. Carroll, I know, is of my opinion about that."

"They don't like Mr. Carroll at Bellevue," said Jeanne. "I've heard several of the men who come there talk about him. It was because of that, because you were in his office, that when I sent Sebastien with the letter to say that I wanted to see you—to tell you about Jacques Latour—I asked you not to come to Bellevue. I didn't want you to come here."

"Apparently someone else didn't want me to come here," Jared said grimly.

There was a moment's silence. Then Jared asked, "Your father will come to the city, now that he knows about this man Latour?"

"I haven't told him about Latour. But he will come, if I urge it. I thought that perhaps I could give French lessons to some of the ladies, and so earn enough to support my father and myself."

"Mrs. Carroll will help," said Jared. "Yes, that's an excellent plan."

"And I can tell Mr. Mellish," went on Jeanne, "that we can't continue to live on his bounty. Oh, my friend, I shall feel so much safer in the town than here in the country!"

"And the Carrolls and I will have you in our special protection," declared Jared. "I would like to see the rascal who would try to harm a friend of Nathaniel Carroll in Philadelphia! He'd find himself in jail like a shot!"

"They are very kind people," murmured Jeanne, "and so are you, Master Jared. And now it's late. Have you a horse?"

"A horse, and a trusty friend, a farmer who's a fighter. Tomorrow I shall talk with Mrs. Carroll, and we'll find a place for you to stay. Send Sebastien to town on some shopping errand, and I'll give him the directions. Then you can make your adieux to Mr. Mellish and snap your fingers at him and his friends."

"Particularly at Mr. Skipworth?"

"Yes, particularly at him, right under his long nose."

There was a bubble of laughter. Then, "Good-night, Master Jared."

"Good-night, Mademoiselle Jeanne." He put out his hand and took her soft fingers, raised them to his lips. "Now you go back to the house. I'll wait here a moment."

She slipped away through the dark. And shortly afterwards Jared stepped out from the trees and walked quickly down the road to where Luke Hatch was waiting.

"All's well?" asked Hatch.

"All's well," responded Jared.

"You'll stop at my house? You must be tired and hungry, and it's some ways yet to the city."

"Nothing would suit me better," said Jared, "than food and a bed."

He untied the mare and climbed into the saddle, and so, riding alongside Hatch's cart, soon found himself at the modest farm-dwelling near the fork in the road.

Hatch's parents, simple, quiet people, made their son's companion feel at home, and, without asking any questions, supplied him with the best food and drink their modest house could provide. Afterwards the young farmer took Jared up to two small bed-rooms under the eaves, one was his own, the other should serve for his guest. There he took the bandage from Jared's head, and from his own experience of cuts and bumps and bruises declared the wounds would heal without any further treatment.

Jared was quickly in bed, and asleep almost as soon as his head touched the pillow.

Greatly refreshed, with a hearty breakfast disposed of, and after many words of thanks to this friend who had aided him so greatly, he took the road with his faithful mare while the grass was still wet with dew next morning. Without further incident he came to Philadelphia, stabled his horse, and sought his room at Mrs. Bird's. There he bathed, put on fresh clothes, and, supplying himself with a hat to take the place of the one he had left at Farmer Powell's, went to Mr. Carroll's office. In his waistcoat pocket he put the gold notched coin that had fallen from Kitt's coat; the pistol he locked in the trunk where he kept his money.

Mr. Carroll was alone in his office when Jared walked in. He gave an exclamation of satisfaction and pushed some papers away. "My dear boy," he said, with unwonted affection, "I was beginning to think you must be in some trouble!"

"I was," said Jared. "I was knocked on the head and taken down the Delaware near to Lewes."

The lawyer's eyes widened. "You don't tell me so, Jared! I found your note, informing me that you'd gone to see Mademoiselle de Severac, accompanied by her servant."

"Shall I tell you my adventures, sir?"

"Most certainly," said Mr. Carroll, waving to a chair.

Jared detailed his story and the lawyer listened without interrupting, his bushy brows lifting several times during the narration, and his thumbs slowly turning over each other, his fingers clasped across his breast.

"And so, if it hadn't been for Luke Hatch," Jared concluded, "I might have been out on the ocean by now, bound Heaven knows where!"

"Most extraordinary!" murmured the lawyer. "That man Hatch was a Godsend!"

"A man in a million, Mr. Carroll! But what does it all mean, sir?"

The lawyer helped himself to a pinch of snuff, flirted his handkerchief, sucked his lips in meditation. "There's something going on in the neighborhood of Bellevue that seems like a criminal conspiracy, Jared. Either they think you know too much about what's in the wind there, or they are afraid you will learn. Of course it has something to do with the misfortunes that are befalling our shipping."

"But I was only concerned with Mademoiselle Jeanne and her father."

"They may not have wanted you to be concerned with Joshua Mellish's guests. Mademoiselle Jeanne was very much frightened at the appearance of this man Latour?"

"Very much, sir. She's convinced he has come here on purpose to harm them."

"A man crazed by the revolution in France... And bringing his new-found ideas of equality to this country. Is it the Marquis or his daughter he's thinking of?"

"But they're penniless, Mr. Carroll. What can such a man want of them?"

The lawyer didn't answer this directly. "When barriers are thrown down the vicious rush in first. And there's no knowing what may be in the mind of a vicious man who finds himself freed from all restraints. Yes, we must bring the Marquis and his daughter to town at once. I'll speak to Mrs. Carroll at dinner in regard to procuring lodgings for them." He reflected a moment. "You heard no names mentioned while you were on the boat or at this Farmer Powell's?"

Jared shook his head. "None, sir."

"And you didn't recognize the man who came aboard the ship in the morning?"

"No, sir." Jared took the gold coin from his pocket. "This is what I found in Kitt's coat; it's like the one the man who boarded the ship had."

Mr. Carroll fingered the coin. " A louis d'or, cut in a singular fashion. A token, no doubt. Yes, Jared, quite innocently you ran afoul of some conspiracy. The question occurs to me: Are the De Severacs, equally innocently, also involved in it? And is it because of your relations to them that the conspirators mistreated you? Is the man Latour allied with these rogues?"

Jared repocketed the coin. "When the De Severacs are safe here I'd like to take a hand in clearing up the river. It ought to be done, Mr. Carroll."

"It undoubtedly calls for attention, Jared. And I don't wonder, after what you've been through, that you take a personal interest in it." The lawyer slapped his hand on the table. "Yes, sir! We can't have pirates at our doors, and that, I'm convinced, is what these fellows are! But we must move cautiously, my boy. With the best intentions in the world Nathaniel Carroll and Jared Lee can't single-handed clear the Delaware of water-snakes."

There, for the time being, the matter stood, their conversation having an interruption in the arrival of a client. But Jared, though he thoroughly appreciated the fact that his preceptor and himself could not proceed, without the aid of the government, to burn out the wasps' nest on the lower river, was not disposed to wait on Mr. Carroll for action. He had seen enough of lawyers and their ways to know how much humming and hawing, arguing pro and con, consideration of precedents, backing and filling and sidestepping were required before they proceeded to get a thing done. Mr. Carroll would probably want to confer with a number of men of his own conservative stamp. From his standpoint that would be right. Jared, however, didn't intend to

sit idle and wait on others' convenience; he meant
to bestir himself.

With this purpose he went, as soon as he had
had a hasty snack at Mrs. Bird's, to the house where
Norroy lodged on High Street above Sixth. A girl
opened the door, and directed him up the stairs, saying that the gentleman was in his room. Jared's
knock was answered by his friend in person, who
in his genial tone invited the caller to enter.

Norroy wore a dressing-gown of maroon wadded
silk, tied by a golden cord. He was smoking a long-
stemmed pipe, and his room was delicately perfumed
by the choicest Virginia tobacco. From an easy
chair he swept a collection of books and gestured
Jared to sit down. "My hour of relaxation and
reflection," he said. "I breakfasted at eleven, and
since have been indulging my taste for the masters
of romance and drama."

"I've a drama to tell you," said Jared. "And then
I want your advice."

Norroy shrugged. "Advice, my dear fellow, as
I find myself frequently reminding you, is not my
strong point. However, I adore drama, and your
manner leads me to believe that I shall find yours
entertaining. Will you smoke?"

Jared shook his head. "Not now." He began
his story.

His legs cocked up on a footstool, his chair tilted
back, Norroy listened with complete attention.

"And if you want proof of what I'm telling you," Jared said as he finished his recital, "there's a lump on the back of my head as big as a turkey's egg and here's the notched louis d'or I found in Bill Kitt's pocket."

Norroy leaned forward and eyed the coin Jared held between thumb and forefinger. "I don't doubt you, my boy. And my advice to you is to throw that thing through the window."

"Indeed I sha'n't," replied Jared, and dropped the coin back in his pocket.

"There, you didn't want advice," said Norroy. "You only wanted to tell me your story."

"I wanted you to tell me what to do. You're a man of experience and Mr. Carroll is only a slow-footed lawyer."

"What to do? Why, thank your stars that you escaped with a whole skin." His smiling eyes regarded the determined face before him. "Remember the amusing, but impractical Spanish Don Quixote, and don't go tilting at windmills; let well enough alone."

"You wouldn't do that if you were in my place," Jared retorted.

"No," Norroy admitted after a moment's thought; "no one ever played me a scurvy trick without my repaying the score. I understand your feeling, Jared. We must make these villains pay."

XIV

THE MISSING COACH

NORROY laid his pipe on a small stand beside his chair, and walking over to an open window stood there for some time, looking out, his hands clasped back of his fine maroon silk dressing-gown. Jared, glancing at the books scattered on the floor, saw that some of them had French titles. As often before, he found himself puzzled by his friend; Norroy seemed to him such a mixture of contradictions; it was difficult to understand how a man of his taste and education and inquiring mind, a man who had seen considerable of the world, could be content with such an indolent existence as he apparently led. He had money, of course, for he lived comfortably, always dressed well, paid his shot at the taverns; but he seemed to have no intimate friends, no business interests, nor any of those concerns that mean so much to an intelligent man.

"You observed a few minutes ago," said Norroy, without turning round, "that I am a man of experience and Mr. Carroll a slow-footed lawyer. I haven't the pleasure of as intimate an acquaintance with Mr. Carroll as you have, but I'm quite willing to take your estimate of him. To the other half

188

of your observation I plead guilty. I *am* a man of considerable experience. I have known a great variety of men. They interest me, especially those the world regards as bad men. Mr. Carroll would put such in jail; I, on the other hand, find that they give spice to existence."

He paused, and from outside came the voice of a huckster calling his fresh vegetables on High Street. Norroy waited until the man had passed by. "I was acquainted early with those Mr. Carroll would probably call loose characters, and I acquired quite an affection for them. They may have been cheats and blacklegs, but they were playing their hand against society, and the odds were a hundred to one that society would best them. I like the under-dog. Damme, Master Jared, I know how the under-dog feels. I had to get out of England, or I'd have been — No, I won't go into that."

"You an under-dog, Hal!"

The man at the window turned. "I don't look like one, eh? More like a proud peacock? Clothes don't matter, my boy, nor a jaunty air, nor a light word. Men have gone to Tyburn with such accompaniments. But all this is beside the question. I should be talking of you and the lovely Mademoiselle Jeanne."

"How is she concerned?"

"Concerned on account of you, Jared," Norroy

replied. "Mademoiselle Jeanne is an uncommonly attractive young lady. Uncommonly attractive young ladies have been known to be the cause of masculine jealousy. Now if it were known to an evil man, who had happened to succumb to the lady's charm, that you stood high in her favor, that you were in fact the particular one on whom she relied for help, is it not conceivable that the evil man might have designs upon you?" Norroy looked at Jared's blank face, and a smile came to his eyes. "You were thinking perhaps of a more complicated explanation for the assault on you? You have hinted at desperadoes and pirates. It does credit to your fancy, Jared. But if there were such men about, what cause would they have to fear you? What knowledge have you of them?"

"Not very much," agreed Jared. "No more, I suppose, than a hundred other people."

"My experience of evil-doers," Norroy continued, "teaches me that they don't go out of their way to knock unimportant people on the head and ship them down the river. Now the only man to whom you might be considered important on the evening you went to Bellevue was the one who was interested in your rendezvous with Mademoiselle Jeanne."

Jared ran his fingers through his hair. "You talk in riddles, Hal. Do you mean this Frenchman Latour who has so frightened her?"

"I hadn't thought of him," answered Norroy. "Though now that you mention him—" He broke off, staring at some new conception. "No," he said after a moment, "I was thinking of Cornelius Skipworth."

"Skipworth! Mademoiselle Jeanne can't abide the sight of him!"

"I am beginning to share her sentiment," said Norroy laconically.

"I detest him," said Jared, "and I'm certain he doesn't like me. But why should he go to such lengths to do me an injury?"

"Skipworth," said Norroy, "is a most unpleasant character. I never encounter his long nose—and you may have noticed that he has a fondness for sticking it into other people's affairs—without wanting to tweak it. I believe he is a man who enjoys doing spiteful acts. His nature is venomous. I have never understood how Mellish could tolerate his company; it may be that he regards Cornelius in the light of a court jester, a mordant wit that delights him by its sting. But we mustn't underestimate Skipworth. If he wanted you out of his way he would find some means to achieve his purpose. And Cornelius, as I happen to know, thinks that he has great powers over the fair sex; the fact that a young lady like Mademoiselle de Severac looks coldly on him today, would, in his estimation, be

no reason whatever why he shouldn't be able to con-
jure her to look warmly on him tomorrow."

"The ugly beast!" exclaimed Jared. "He'd never
be able to do that!"

"You know a great deal about the ladies, don't
you?" said Norroy, amusement in his eye. "You
may be right in this particular case, though I don't
believe you'd ever be able to get Skipworth to agree
with you." He walked the length of the room,
swinging the gold tassel of the cord to his dressing-
gown. "Skipworth is your enemy; possibly he began by disliking you because you were so different
from himself—so evidently honest and straightfor-
ward—and then you beat him at cards that evening
at Mellish's party, and afterwards knocked him
down, and finally there is this blue-eyed French
girl who prefers your friendship to his. He learned
she had sent you a message, he knew you proposed
a rendezvous on the bank of the river; and he
hired some bullies to make off with you. A high-
handed proceeding undoubtedly, but a manner of
getting rid of unwanted people that is practised in
the best English and Continental society today."

"But I can't prove that," objected Jared. "I
have nothing to show that it was actually Skipworth,
though it may have been he."

"The student of law again, with his need of
proof!" rallied Norroy. "Leave that to me, my

son. I know a great deal about Cornelius. I have
a score of my own to settle with this hatchet-faced,
nosey gentleman, and I'll add your item to the total."

"But I don't want to place you in hazard on my
account," objected Jared. "I can fight my own battles. From what you say Skipworth has bullies
under his orders, and he might do you harm."

"He's welcome to try it," answered Norroy. "I
can bite as well as he." From serious his mood,
always varying, always shifting as quicksilver,
changed to mischief again. "Jared, my chief joy
in life is encountering hazards. I court them as
the lover courts the face of his lady. You see me
here, lolling at ease, and reading the great romances.
I read them because I would lead such magnificent
adventurous lives myself; and haply some day I may.
You think you know Hal Norroy, but take my word
for it you don't. My stay in your good Quaker
City is simply a marking time; I find a certain pleasure in it, since it brings me your acquaintance; but
I shall fly away again to wider, wilder scenes. And
meantime, for fault of better occupation, I shall
pull Skipworth's nose."

On that pleasing assurance Jared rose and left
his mystifying friend. He pondered what Norroy
had said and also other angles of the problem that
was presented to him, and his conclusion was that
his most immediate concern was to have the Marquis

13

and his daughter settled in the city. To further that purpose he called in the evening on the Carrolls.

The lawyer had already talked with his wife, and Jared learned that Mrs. Carroll had interested herself in the business with her customary energy. She had seen a Mrs. Derbyshire, who had two bedrooms and a sitting-room for rent, and who would supply meals, and had tentatively engaged these accommodations. She said, moreover, that she would be glad to have Mademoiselle Jeanne give French lessons to Elizabeth and Hannah, and had spoken to several friends about the desirability of having the Marquis's daughter instruct their children in that polite tongue. When Mrs. Carroll took an enterprise in hand its success was assured, and Jared departed from her house feeling that the De Severacs had secured a pleasant haven.

The next day Sebastien came to town in the chaise hired at the Green Anchor and stopped at Mr. Carroll's office. Jared told him the plans for his master and young mistress; they should leave Bellevue the following day and drive to Philadelphia, there they would call on Mrs. Carroll and she would introduce them to Mrs. Derbyshire. The matter was simple enough, and the faithful old servant showed his satisfaction at the plan. "My young lady hasn't been happy in Mr. Mellish's big house, Mr. Lee," he said. "I think she'll very much prefer the society in the city."

"Mr. Skipworth is still at Bellevue?" Jared asked.

"Yes, sir, he is there. There's plenty of company for Mademoiselle Jeanne, but she keeps mostly to herself."

"Well, after tomorrow she can choose her own friends," said Jared, "and I think she'll find the people here more congenial than Mr. Mellish's guests."

The following day Jared was constantly glancing through the window, and whenever he left the office on some errand for Mr. Carroll he loitered on the street, looking for a chaise or a coach bearing the Marquis and his daughter to town. If they started in the morning they should arrive by mid-afternoon; but four o'clock passed, and then five, without a glimpse of them. Mr. Carroll finished his work for the day, and left for the stroll he was in the habit of taking to refresh himself. Jared found the Carrolls' man-servant trimming the hedge that bordered the walk to their front door, and asked him if any carriage had arrived that afternoon, to be informed that none had.

The fancy took him to get his roan and the pistol of Bill Kitt and ride to meet the De Severacs, who must come by the highroad from Bellevue, cross the lower ferry and follow Second Street to the centre of

town. This was quickly accomplished; he inquired at
the ferry concerning travellers from the south, but
learned of none that answered the description of those
he was interested in; and, crossing the river, rode
into the country.

The setting sun found him still riding, eagerly
scanning the distance for a chaise or a coach. He
met an occasional farm-wagon or a horseman. He
began to wonder if something might have happened
at Bellevue to cause the De Severacs to change their
plans, to postpone their journey to the next day.
By now he meant to push on and find out. His
horse, that had not been exercised for several days,
was fresh and willing.

It was starlight when he neared his goal. He decided that it would not do for him to present himself
at Bellevue too impatiently, and so he continued on
to the Green Anchor Inn. Inquiry at the stables
elicited the information that no chaise had been hired
that day. He went into the tavern and had a bite
of supper, exchanging a word or two with Simeon
Oakes about the fine weather.

Presently he determined to ride up the drive to
Bellevue, his excuse for a call a message from Mr.
Carroll to the Marquis regarding a letter just received bearing on conditions in France. He fastened
his horse to the hitching-post and rapped with the
big brass knocker. Admitted, he found himself after

a few minutes greeting Joshua Mellish in the drawing-room.

"I'm right glad to see you, Mr. Lee," said Mellish. "It's always a pleasure to welcome a friend. May I offer you a glass of wine?"

"No, thank you, sir," said Jared. "I have some information about the state of affairs in France that Mr. Carroll thought might interest the Marquis."

"And doubtless it would," agreed Mellish with his ready smile. "But the Marquis and his daughter took leave of me today. They went to Philadelphia. I urged them to stay; their presence here has been a great pleasure to me, but they had their own reasons for preferring the town."

Jared stared at the round, red face of the master of Bellevue. "You say, Mr. Mellish, that they left your house today? If you'll pardon my seeming inquisitive, at what hour did they depart?"

"About three in the afternoon. They should be in the city long before this, Mr. Lee. The Marquis suggested that he would engage a carriage at the inn, but I wouldn't hear of it. My stables are always at the disposition of my friends; I begged them to make use of my coach and pair of bays; I told them I should be much offended if they did anything else."

"I've recently come from town," said Jared, "and I didn't meet them on the road. Your coach wouldn't have reached the ferry till after six, and I'd crossed the river by that time."

"You should have met them," Mellish stated. "My own man, Peter Collins, was driving, and he's a trusty fellow "

"Who travelled with them?" asked Jared. "Their servant, Sebastien, I fancy—and possibly Mr. Skipworth?"

"Their servant, yes. But not Cornelius; he left here early this morning."

"It's a straight road, and they had a reliable driver," said Jared, thinking aloud. "I don't understand why I didn't meet them."

"Nor do I," agreed Mellish. "But, Mr. Lee, we'll find there's some simple explanation. A horse may have cast a shoe, and they have stopped at a smithy. Your concern does you credit, sir; your interest in the Marquis and his daughter is easy to understand; I esteem them immensely; we would not have such distinguished guests suffer any inconvenience. They have been delayed somewhere perhaps, but by now they must surely be in Philadelphia."

There was nothing to which Jared could take exception in Mellish's expression or manner. He was clearly solicitous as to the welfare of his recent guests, even though that solicitude did not appear to sit heavily on his shoulders. Now he stepped to a bell-rope. "You must have a glass of wine, Mr.

Lee. And after that, since I see that you have this puzzle on your mind, I won't seek to detain you. Rest assured you will find the Marquis and his daughter safely arrived in town."

A servant brought Madeira and Jared drank a glass. Afterwards, with more words of assurance from Mellish, he took his leave, mounted the roan and turned into the highroad. He saw no reason to doubt what Joshua Mellish had told him, and yet he felt concerned. The man Latour was in the neighborhood, and there was also Skipworth, and either of them might make trouble for the De Severacs.

It was after midnight when his tired horse brought Jared back to the city, too late an hour for him to rouse the Carrolls or to break in on Mrs. Derbyshire. Perforce he had to seek his room and go to bed, hoping that in the morning he would learn that the Marquis and Jeanne were safely ensconced in their new lodgings.

Morning, however, brought no such information. The De Severacs had not arrived at Mr. Carroll's door, neither had they presented themselves to Mrs. Derbyshire. Nothing had been seen of Joshua Mellish's coach, though Jared made inquiry at all the better class of taverns. He talked with Mr. Carroll, telling him of his visit to Bellevue on the previous evening, and the lawyer bent his brows in a portentous frown and took several pinches of snuff.

"Disappeared, eh?" said he. "It's most unaccountable, Jared. They left Mellish's place at three yesterday afternoon? You have his word for that. I doubt the rascal; and yet what purpose could he have in injuring this peaceful gentleman and his daughter?"

"I don't think Mr. Mellish would injure them," said Jared. "I think he genuinely likes them."

"If he's done them a harm, we'll make him pay for it," declared Mr. Carroll. "I consider them under my protection."

Words were not what Jared wanted, and when he saw that his preceptor had nothing more definite to suggest he went out on the street and watched the roads that led up from the ferry. At noon he went back to Mrs. Bird's, and his landlady handed him a letter.

"A boy brought this from the City Tavern," she explained. "He said it came by one of the morning coaches."

Jared looked at the envelope, wondering if by any chance it might be from Jeanne. His name, however, was written in a bold script, masculine, not a lady's.

He tore the envelope open and took out the folded

sheet. The signature was "Hal Norroy," penned with a dashing flourish. He read the message:

"Dear Jared: I have gone about the business we discussed in my room. I think I shall come up with the gentleman very soon. I am writing this at a table at the Inn of the Three Pigeons, a dirty hole, but one that suits the taste of the gentleman you wot of. A glass of French brandy sits on the table near to my ink-pot, and I think when the gentleman comes in I shall fling it into his face. I should like to see it run dripping down that long nose. Perchance, however, I shall think of some more engaging method of maddening him. In any case I shall settle the score for you and for myself.

"I am weary of well doing in your quiet town, and think to emulate the example of some of my favorite heroes. If we never meet again, keep me in your recollection. May you rise to be Chief Justice, or whatever stands at the apex of your noble profession!"

Jared went up to his room, and unlocking his trunk provided himself with money. Norroy's note set spurs to his mounting impatience. He was going to find out what had happened to the passengers in Mellish's coach.

XV

INQUIRIES ON THE ROAD

THE rotund, red-faced proprietor of the Pig and Whistle Tavern, a place of entertainment a mile south of Philadelphia on the Chester Road, was sitting on his porch—there being no customers in his taproom—enjoying a pipe and the afternoon sun when there appeared before him a well-built young man in a suit of excellent brown broadcloth. With an effort and a grunt the barrel-figured proprietor got to his feet. "A warm day, sir, and a dusty one too," he observed, his gesture indicating the open door, through which might be seen a row of shining pewter tankards hanging on the wall.

"I'll have a glass of ale here," said Jared Lee, "and I'd be glad if you'd fetch one for yourself." From his purse he took a new-minted coin and dropped it on the innkeeper's pudgy palm.

The proprietor waddled away, and soon was back with the order. Seeing that the young gentleman desired his society he sat down and took a long drink. "You'll not find better than that anywhere in the city," he remarked with satisfaction. "A prime ale, sir; full-bodied, but not too heavy. I know ale, and I only serve the best."

202

"It's very good," nodded Jared; and, having established a friendly footing with the fat proprietor, who he saw was of a talkative nature, he disclosed his business. "I've been expecting some friends of mine, a gentleman and a young lady, to arrive in Philadelphia either yesterday or today. They haven't appeared, however, and as they are supposed to be travelling over this road by private coach I've set out to look for them. Have you chanced to see any such travellers?"

"An elderly gentleman in black and the young lady his daughter?" queried the proprietor. "Aye, sir, they were here no longer ago than last evening. They ate their supper in my dining-room."

"Ah," said Jared, "I'm glad you can tell me of them. I wonder they didn't drive on to supper in the city."

"One of their horses went lame," explained the innkeeper. "A stone in its shoe cut the foot. There was no one here at the time who could tend to it and we had to send for the smith."

"What time did they arrive here?"

"About sundown it was. And being delayed on account of the smith they ordered supper. I served the lady and gentleman myself in the dining-room, and their servant and the coachman ate in the kitchen. It was dark before they left, nigh on to nine o'clock."

"They were going to Philadelphia?" Jared asked.

"So I heard them say."

"Did you learn their names?"

"The servant called the gentleman by some foreign title, French I think it was—Mounseer de—"

"Severac?" suggested Jared.

"Aye, it sounded like that. Tongue-twisting names foreigners have."

Jared set down his glass on the porch. "Who was in your stable when the coach arrived?"

"Only the stable boy, sir. He knows naught of shoeing horses."

"I'd like a word with him."

The innkeeper led the way to the stable, shouting "Hullo, Joe, hullo!"

A spindling, carrot-topped lad appeared. "This gentleman wants to ask about the coach that was here yester-night," said the boy's master.

"The horse with a stone in its shoe," Jared supplemented. "Was the foot much cut?"

"I didn't see it," said the boy. "I went to fetch the smith. He tended to the horse."

"You don't know how bad the hurt was?" Jared continued.

The boy shook his head. "The coachman said it was pretty bad. But the smith made it right again, sir. I went out to the road and watched when they drove away, and that horse stepped out very easy."

"You saw the coach drive north toward Philadelphia?"

"Why, no, sir, it didn't go north. It headed south from here, I saw it swing out into the Milldam Road."

"South!" exclaimed Jared. "Where does the Milldam Road lead?"

"It makes a big loop and comes back to the turnpike four or five miles below here," explained the innkeeper. "That's odd, ain't it, sir? Looks as if your friends had changed their minds about going to the city."

"The lady and gentleman and their servant were in the coach and it was dark outside," said Jared, thinking aloud. "They may not have noticed in which direction they were being driven." He turned abruptly on his heel. "Very well. I'll have to look for them somewhere south of here." And striding off to his roan he mounted and trotted off, leaving the proprietor and boy of the Pig and Whistle staring after him.

There had been some chicanery practised, Jared felt certain, though for what object he could not surmise. He did not believe that the Marquis had ordered the coachman to drive south instead of toward the town, and he could understand how Jeanne, her father, and Sebastien, seated in the coach, not very familiar with the road, and only glimpsing it

—if indeed they looked out at all—in the darkness, would have taken it for granted that they were travelling north, relying on the trustworthiness of Mr. Mellish's driver.

To Jared, however, suspicion was now a confidant, whispering continually in his ear. Had one of the coach-horses actually picked up a stone and so caused a delay from sundown until after nightfall? The stable boy hadn't seen the injured hoof, only the coachman and the smith they had sent for. The smith might have been induced, for a silver coin, to see whatever the coachman told him to see, and to take his time over the business.

There had been trickery evidently, and Mellish's servant had been an agent in it. Thoroughly aroused now, fearful of what might have befallen, hot with indignant anger, determined to right the matter, Jared rode post-haste to the door of Bellevue.

Mellish was walking in his garden, and there Jared came to him. "Mr. Mellish," said Jared, "the Marquis and his daughter haven't been seen in town. Where is the coachman that drove them?"

"I don't know," answered Mellish. "He hasn't returned. I made inquiry about him."

Jared stared at the pink-cheeked man, and under his glance the latter lost something of his amiable manner. A scowl came to his brow and his face flushed. "You are excited, Mr. Lee," he remonstrated. "Allow me to point out to you that excitement accomplishes little."

"This coachman of yours was a man you trusted?" Jared demanded.

"I trust all my servants, sir."

"But neither the man nor the coach have returned to Bellevue?"

"Neither," said Mellish, and shrugged his shoulders. "You know as much concerning what has happened to them as I do myself."

Jared bit his lips to keep from speaking hotly; nothing was to be gained by making Mellish angry. "I know something," he said on a more even note. "The coachman stopped at an inn a little this side of the ferry; it appears, to believe what he told the stable boy, that one of the horses had picked up a stone and cut its foot. This caused a considerable delay, so long in fact that the Marquis and his daughter took their supper at the tavern, the Pig and Whistle, and didn't leave until some time after dark. But when they did leave the stable boy tells me the coachman didn't drive on toward town, but took a road to the south."

"I don't understand his purpose," said Mellish, who appeared frankly puzzled, "unless the Marquis had changed his plans and gave him other orders. In that case my man would undoubtedly have obeyed them."

"But where could he have wished to go? They didn't return to your house, and they have no friends in this part of the country. If they had gone to any house in the neighborhood, your man would have been here by now."

Mellish clasped his hands behind his back and looked with a troubled eye at the young fellow. "I can't answer your question, Mr. Lee. I wish I could, for I'd not have any harm come to those two people! What is your own conjecture?"

"That your coachman is a villain, Mr. Mellish."

Mellish paled, unclasped his hands, fingered a button on his coat. "You use strong words, Mr. Lee. However, I'll not quarrel with you. What's to be done now?"

"The man was in the pay of other villains. Who would profit by laying hands on the Marquis and his daughter?"

"They had some money with them. There have been reports of robbers."

"There has been a Frenchman, Latour, in the neighborhood," said Jared; "an enemy of your guests. Have you heard of him?"

"I have heard of no such person," Mellish replied in his most positive manner.

"And there have been reports of lawlessness all through this country," Jared went on; "from here down to the Capes, of brigandage and high-handed business. If you've not heard of the state of this neighborhood you're the only man hereabouts who's still in ignorance."

"You amaze me!" said Mellish. "I wonder some-one hasn't told me. Cornelius now—he usually knows what's going on." He shook his head. "I live here simply, with my flowers and my trees, en-tertaining my friends, thinking ill of no one. . . . And now you come, Mr. Lee, and tell me of all manner of alarms!"

Was the man really the fatuous fool he made himself out to be, the honey-pot around which such flies as Skipworth buzzed; or was he an active part-ner in the evil that went on along the river? Jared couldn't determine. "Well, now that you have heard," he stated abruptly, "you'll understand why I'm so much concerned about the Marquis and his daughter."

"And I too," said Mellish quickly. "I am greatly concerned. I put myself and everyone in my house at your service in trying to find them."

Since he could think of no immediate way in which to make use of Mellish and his household— there being also some question in his mind as to the master of Bellevue's own innocence of roguery —Jared declined this proffer. "Pray do as you think best, sir," he said. "You must have some means of informing yourself concerning the affairs of your missing coachman; his family or friends should be able to help you there.   Mr. Carroll is making the cause of the Marquis his own, and will prosecute any guilty persons.   Good-afternoon." A jerky bow, and Jared turned away.

Mellish said something, but Jared paid no attention to him.   He despised this sleek, well-fed man and suspected him of being a hypocrite.   A man who would tolerate Skipworth must be easily fooled, or else—or else shared some interest with Skipworth for their mutual benefit.

A backward glance showed Jared that Mellish had seated himself in the summerhouse.   Going to his horse Jared walked the roan around to the stable, where a groom was furbishing a set of harness. The man recognized Jared as a former guest at Bellevue, and touched finger to forelock.   "You might be wanting something, sir?" he inquired.

"Mr. Mellish tells me that his coach hasn't returned from Philadelphia," said Jared.   "What was the coachman's name?"

"Ben Hatton," answered the groom.   "He's a right trusty man."

Jared took a dollar from his purse and held it between thumb and finger.   "Has Hatton a family in the neighborhood?"

"No, sir.   He's a single man," said the groom, his eye on the dollar.   "He's been in the master's service half a year or so, and there's never been any complaint of him, so far as I've heard."

Jared reflected a moment, then turned to his horse.

"Ben is well thought of, sir," continued the groom. "Yesterday morning I saw Mr. Skipworth give him a present. Mr. Skipworth's very generous, sir."

The dollar twinkled again as Jared turned. "Mr. Skipworth left here yesterday morning, didn't he?"

"Early it was, sir," nodded the groom. "He came to the stable for his horse, and it was then I saw him talking to Ben."

"Did Mr. Skipworth say where he was going?"

The groom's eyes met Jared's, and the latter tossed the coin into the man's palm. "Mr. Skipworth doesn't say much, sir," came the answer; "but I've a notion he might have been going down to the Three Pigeons."

Norroy's inn! The place mentioned in his letter!

"Where is that?" asked Jared.

"A mile or two this side o' Lewes." The groom gave a sly wink. "Excellent brandy it has, sir. Some say that it comes in from France with no questions asked."

"What makes you think Mr. Skipworth might have gone there?"

But the groom didn't care to give a reason. "He's a sporting gentleman, sir. And he has many odd friends."

Jared noted the sly look and took the hint. "A good place to stay away from, if one isn't as well known as Mr. Skipworth?" he asked lightly.

"Why, so I think," grinned the groom. "There's good brandy to be had short of the Three Pigeons."

"I can do without it," said Jared, and put his foot in the stirrup.

The Inn of the Three Pigeons! There Norroy had gone when he set out to look for Skipworth; and to that fact was now added the hint of Mellish's groom. That the Frenchman Latour had had a hand in the disappearance of Jeanne and her father was hardly credible, but that Skipworth was the fount of their misfortune was being borne ever more forcibly in upon Jared's thoughts.

His lips tightened in a straight line as he rode his horse through the sunset afterglow. And when he came to the crossroads north he turned toward Luke Hatch's cottage.

A sturdy figure swung through a nearby field at sight of him, and a lusty voice gave him welcome. "Master Lee, were you looking for me?" asked Hatch as he approached.

The roan was stabled. The two went indoors, and there Jared told his friend the story of the missing coach. "And now," finished Jared, "I mean to go to this tavern of the Three Pigeons, near to

Lewes, and find what Skipworth is about, if Norroy has left him a tongue to answer my questions."

Hatch smiled. "You're a rare one, master. But I doubt you can handle such a man alone. Let me go along of you, and then, if there's a fight, I'll be at your elbow. I've heard tell of the Three Pigeons. It's got an ill name; but if you've a mind to go there let me go along of you."

"I don't want you to come to any trouble. I only wanted someone, some friend, to know where I was going."

"Trouble!" cried Hatch. "I'm growing fat with farming. I need a little trouble of this kind to keep my eye in trim." He slapped his knee and laughed. "I'm your man, master. You stay here tonight, and tomorrow at sun-up we'll go jogging. Bless you, Master Lee, we'll set this business right in no time! My word on it, sir!"

XVI

THE INN OF THE THREE PIGEONS

THE sun had not much more than cleared the horizon next morning when two horsemen, one mounted on a roan, the other on a bay, swung out from the Hatch farmstead and turned their faces south. Overhead was a clear sky, and in the air was the magic perfume of early summer, that soft but heady compound of essences distilled by warmth from bud and bloom and fruit. Birds sang in the fields and soared from nests in the thickets. Along either side of the road was a tangle of fresh green and clusters of wild flowers.

On such a day anything might be accomplished; that was the song in the ears of Jared and Luke. Better than driving a plow was this to Hatch, and he said so often to his companion, who nodded and smiled. Jared's emotions in the adventure were more mixed; there was the question of the safety of his French friends, which was sobering; but there was also action, which stirred his senses and appealed to his strength.

Hatch knew the country well, and they stopped at noon at the house of a friend of his, where they were welcomed to dinner. That night they slept at a tavern, located where the Smyrna River and Duck Creek flowed into the Delaware. Next morning they were again early afoot and to horse, and now as they rode they had on their left the wide sweep of water, broadening and broadening out to the Capes and the Atlantic Ocean.

By afternoon they were in a country where hamlets were few and farmhouses distant from each other, a fertile country and fair, with the breath of the sea over it, rimmed on the east with salt marshes and tidal creeks, a land of sailors as well as of farmers.

They asked a passing drover the distance to the Three Pigeons, and, being answered, decided they could, by pressing on, reach it by nightfall. With the setting sun a mist blew up from the water, which cooled their faces and freshened their tired horses. Presently they eased their pace, the road being none too good. The sun set and twilight softened the country. Now the air was damp and of a salty savor.

The road grew dusky ahead. They picked their way carefully. Wraiths of fog blew across their faces, veils that swept up from the water and floated away to the west. Darkness settled on the country, but the two rode on, and finally, as reward for their perseverance, a path of light that was like a yellow ribbon streamed over the road just beyond.

Approaching, they were able by the light to distinguish the outlines of a low, straggling building, close to the road, and by its appearance a public-house. Jared and Hatch had already discussed their plans, and now, dismounting, they tied their horses in a thicket on the landward side of the road, and walked over toward the building. On nearer view it was not prepossessing. Bushes grew close to its walls and the ground in front was uncleared. The front door was closed, but the light that shone out from the northern windows on the lower floor showed the house was inhabited.

The two skirted the door, and, rounding the corner, stood in the bushes on a level with the windows. They were looking into a taproom, where a lamp hung above the bar. And near the window through which Hatch and Jared were gazing two men, at the moment the only occupants of the room, were seated at a table, glasses before them, talking earnestly.

One was Cornelius Skipworth, the other a much heavier, less elegantly-garbed fellow, with forward-thrusting shoulders and a great shock of hair.

Jared whispered the name of Skipworth into Hatch's ear.

The two in the room sat with their backs to the window, facing the door. Skipworth's companion was drawing patterns on the table with his forefinger, moistened with drippings from his glass, while he listened to what the other said.

Hatch tried the lower window-frame, pressing it at several places, at the bottom, the sides, the top. The frame was old and warped and loose, and could be easily raised. Stepping aside, Hatch took a knife from his pocket, and in a moment had cut a short stick from a sapling. This he wedged under the lower frame of the window, and very cautiously, without making any noise, pushed it gently up.

Neither man in the room seemed to notice what had happened; but now their voices came distinctly to the listeners outside.

At first Jared made little of the drift of the conversation, but presently Skipworth's companion laid a finger on the other's sleeve. "Enough of this talk," he declared. "I'm with you about the Captain. He's not to be relied on."

"Too much of a parson," sneered Skipworth.

The other man threw back his head. "You'd not say that to his face!" he retorted. "Not if you value your skin."

"I'll speak him my mind when I choose," said Skipworth. "I'm watching for the right chance."

The burly man turned his head a trifle, so that Jared saw he had a beak of a nose and an out-thrust, upward-reaching chin, something like that of Punchinello in the puppet shows. "Wait till we lay hands on this brig," he said. "I know the Captain, and I know when to take him. The crew'll do his bidding when the devil's in him; but when he's slack and moody—" The speaker nodded and jabbed Skipworth's sleeve with his stubby finger; "then's the time to get him."

"The brig will be coming down the river any time now," Skipworth said, moving his arm away from the other's finger. "She may be the last prize. The merchants are mounting guns."

"There's more ways than one to steal a cargo," observed his companion dryly. "I've known the right man aboard a ship to outwit all the officers and crew."

Skipworth drained his glass. "Doubtless there is always a way to turn an honest penny," he remarked in his sardonic tone. "And the fewer there are to share the coins, Rand, the more there are for each."

"Aye," agreed the other. "Well, the Captain don't need his share as much as the rest of us."

"I'll stay till you've settled with him," declared Skipworth. "I have business to attend to here, the shipping of cargoes to the West Indies."

He rapped on the table, and, after a moment, a door behind the bar opened and a man in an apron came in.

Skipworth handed the man some money and, rising, took his hat from a peg on the wall. "I'll walk along with you, Rand," he said to his companion, and moved toward the front door.

Jared and Hatch, in the bushes at the corner of the tavern, saw the two men emerge and turn into the road toward the south.

Back at the window again they found that the innkeeper had left the room, and Hatch, removing the stick that had propped the frame, allowed the glass to drop noiselessly into place.

"As nice a pair of cutthroats," muttered Hatch, "as I've ever laid my eyes on."

"Skipworth is here," said Jared, "but what's become of my friend, Norroy?"

"And the two of us be here," said Hatch, "but what's for us to do now?"

"The horses need bedding," said Jared.

"Aye, that they do." Hatch pondered shortly. "This here is a public-house, and there's not like to be another for many a mile."

"I shouldn't like to meet Skipworth," said Jared, "until I find Norroy; but maybe Skipworth won't be back. If he meant to sleep at the inn doubtless he'd not have left."

So, induced by the necessity of caring for the tired beasts that had served them so loyally, the two led their horses up to the tavern door. The

travellers went in, and at sound of their entrance
the man in the apron appeared.

He was a dark, untidy person, with eyes that
shifted continually and a loose, thick-lipped mouth.
His manner was distinctly surly, and when Jared said
they wanted a room for the night and food and
stabling for their horses he shook his head. "I've
got no room for strangers," he said. "I was just
shutting up for the night. You'll have to go some-
wheres else."

"But the horses are footsore and tired, and there
isn't another public-house within ten miles," objected Jared.

The innkeeper shook his head, his eyes not on
the two who stood before him, but on the open door
behind them.

Jared put his hand in his pocket. The sight of
money might shake the man's obstinacy. His fingers
touched a loose coin and he drew it out. "You shall
be paid in advance," he said, holding up the piece
of money.

The innkeeper's glance, shifting from the door,
focussed on the coin that Jared presented, and his
lips, that had opened to utter another surly refusal,
made a round O of surprise instead.

Jared saw that by chance he had fished from his
pocket the gold louis d'or with the four nicks cut
in its rim. But since the innkeeper seemed much

interested in it, Jared continued to hold it so the man might see his fill.

"Hm—m," said the innkeeper, closing his thick lips. His beady eyes shifted for a second to Jared's face, then back to the gold piece. "So that's the pay you offer? Why didn't you show it first?"

Jared smiled good-humoredly. "Come, that puts a different look on the question whether you'll take us in or not, doesn't it? You shall be well paid for lodging us and our horses. But not with that particular piece; with good American money." And, dropping the louis d'or into the palm of his other hand, he returned it to his pocket.

The innkeeper grunted assent. "You can stay," he muttered. "I'll fetch a lantern."

With the lantern he was presently showing Hatch and Jared around to a stable at the rear. There oats were provided for the horses and a couple of straw-bedded stalls.

The animals attended to, the three returned to the taproom, where the innkeeper, with a grumble, shot the bolt in the front door.

"You're not expecting more customers tonight?" said Jared, thinking of the possibility of encountering Skipworth.

"I wouldn't open that door for the Devil himself!" declared the man. "I've been up since cockcrow, and you're the last two I take in!"

"A bite of supper," suggested Jared; "and you can get to bed."

Food—such as it was—was set before the travellers; salt pork and cold, greasy potatoes, washed down by foaming ale. With appetites made voracious by their long ride they quickly cleared their plates while the innkeeper, flopped in a near-by chair, regarded them with baleful eye.

Candle in hand, the man led them up a flight of creaking stairs to a room with two beds under the eaves. He placed the candle on a bare pine table, and with a grunt that was intended for good-night left them to themselves.

They waited until the innkeeper's footsteps had creaked away in the distance, then Hatch opened the door and peered out. Shutting it again, he whispered to Jared, "There's no one hiding there. The rat's gone to bed."

A colloquy in whispers followed and a look around the room. There was only one door and one window, the door without bolt or key, the window without a catch. As quietly as they were able the two lifted one of the beds so that its high headboard stood across the window and, pulling a chest in front of the door, piled the table and a couple of chairs on top of it.

"If any one breaks in here tonight," chuckled Hatch, "he'll make enough noise to let us know he's coming. But I think we'll be snug till morning, Master Lee. 'Twas that gold-piece of yours that did the business."

"What do you make of this place?" Jared asked in a whisper.

"Thieves' den. We're in their proper country. Remember what that rascally gentleman said. There's a brig coming down the river, and they mean to get her."

"But what about the Marquis and his daughter and Norroy?" asked Jared.

Hatch shook his head. "We'll have a look for them tomorrow. We're in rogue's country, and no mistake."

Jared put his pistol in easy reach of his hand, and climbed into bed. For a long time he lay awake. Then he thought he heard a scratching at the window behind his bed. He crouched and, looking over the headboard, saw—or thought he saw—a face gazing in. Immediately it disappeared. With pistol gripped and ears alert for any sounds within the house or out he settled down again.

XVII

ADVENTURE ON THE BEACH

No ONE broke in on them that night. They rose at dawn and discussed their plans. Their business now was to learn whether the Marquis and his daughter were to be found in the country that stretched along the Delaware to the Atlantic Ocean. Also Jared was anxious to know what had happened to Norroy, and if by any chance the latter had become involved in the fate of his French friends. It was easier to state the purpose of the search, however, than to know how to go about it. The country in which Jared and Hatch found themselves was very sparsely populated; there were a few scattered farms, and farther down the coast the little village of Lewes, the home of some fishermen and sailors, a collection of straggling houses.

The innkeeper of the Three Pigeons was not a man to be questioned. He was neither more loquacious nor more agreeable in the morning than he had been at night. He served breakfast to his customers and took their directions concerning the horses, but with an air that implied he did so only on sufferance. A glance at his small, roving eyes was enough to show that any requests for information would be met with duplicity, if not with forthright lying, and in all probability the questions asked would be repeated to some of his intimates at the first convenient moment.

The best attitude to take with him, therefore, seemed to be that the travellers knew their own business and needed no assistance in the going about it. Adopting this course, Jared told him, when they had finished breakfast, that they would leave the horses in his stable for the present, paid him what was owed, dismissed him with a gesture, and with Hatch went out at the tavern door.

There had been a change in the weather overnight, and the sunlight was thin and watery, with great banks of clouds driving up from the south. The river, which lay not more than fifty yards from the Three Pigeons, was greenish-blue and of a metallic sheen. The air was chill and damp. This was a sea country, sandy, marshy, and open, except where a line of dark green woods rimmed a ridge to the west.

Jared and Hatch tramped southward all that morning and found only a few farmers, who could tell them nothing of such a coach as Mellish's or of its occupants. At noon, on the outskirts of Lewes, they procured dinner through the offices of a friendly blacksmith, who took them to his house. Afterwards they walked through the village, and tarried

15

for some time on the waterfront, but the men with whom they chanced to talk were uncommunicative, and only interested in the weather, their boats, and the price to be had for fish.

Baffled, with no clues to follow, the two took the road north again as the afternoon sun hid itself in a bed of amethyst clouds. Jared, his hands in his pockets, shook his head moodily. "I'm about ready to think that the Marquis and his daughter never came as far down the river as this," he said; "but Norroy wrote to me from the Three Pigeons and we saw Skipworth there, and what's become of them? Skipworth was here on business, but where did his business take him?"

" 'Tis a wide country," said Hatch, "and we've seen only this road and yon small village. This road, if you mark it, doesn't follow the river for some distance this side of Lewes, it takes a short cut inland, with woods on the Delaware side. And there's all yon land to the westward, miles and miles of it. 'Twould be easy to lose a score of people 'twixt the east and west of us."

Jared agreed to that. "We must search another day," he said, and plodded stolidly along.

They had come so far south, however, that waning daylight still found them some miles from the tavern. Chilly twilight wrapped the road, foretokening early darkness. Presently Hatch slowed up. "There's nothing to be gained by supping at the inn, is there, master? If we come late, there's less chance of falling in with Skipworth or his mates."

Jared glanced about. This was a lonely section, with woods to the right and bare fields to the left. "What were you thinking, Luke?"

"There's a house ahead. Might we ask for a bit of supper?"

Jared saw the farmhouse through the gray light. "That suits me. I don't want to fall in with Skipworth."

A knock on the door brought a bearded man, and a request to purchase food was answered affirmatively. The strangers were given seats at the supper table, already occupied by the farmer's wife and four children. Silent at first, the four soon broke through their shyness, and Jared and Hatch ate to the accompaniment of shrill chatter.

After supper the man went with the strangers to his door. It was now dark outside and clouds hid the stars. "Where ye bound?" asked the man. "It's some walk to Lewes."

"We're making for the Three Pigeons," answered Jared.

"Some walk there too," was the comment. "You should make it in a couple of hours."

"We can't miss the road, can we?" inquired Hatch.

"No, there's only the one road. It comes out on the river about a mile north of here."

"And what's over there?" asked Hatch, pointing to the woods that fronted the cottage.

"The Delaware," said the farmer. "But take my advice and don't go prowling along that bit of shore. Stick to the road. That's the safest plan in this part of the country."

On they went through the darkness. And presently Jared, at one side of the highway, stopped and muttered: "Luke, here's a path; no, it's a wagon road, wide enough to drive through. I suppose it goes down to the river."

"Likely enough it does," agreed Hatch.

Jared stood there, thoughtfully.

"We've got to search this country, Luke. And better in the dark than the daylight."

"It's dark," chuckled Hatch. "But I've followed a road through the woods by the feel of its ruts before now." He turned off to the right. "Keep close behind me, Master Lee."

The trees met about them. There was only the scuffle of feet for some time. Then, as the path abruptly branched in a new direction, Hatch halted and exclaimed, "Yon's the Delaware!"

Jared stepped beside his companion, but even as his eyes tried to pierce the darkness, a hand caught his arm and twisted it backward, so that he gave a sharp cry of pain.

"There!" said a man's voice, "stop your squealing, or I'll bash you over the head!"

And another voice spoke beside Hatch. "Easy, my lad, easy! I've a pistol here, and my finger's on the trigger!"

Two men stood before Hatch and Jared, each with a pistol in his hand.

"What do you want?" Jared demanded. "Don't try to wrench my arm off!"

"What are you doing here?" inquired one of the men.

"We've been down to Lewes," said Jared, trying to think of some excuse for their presence in the woods.

"Who are you, and where were you going?" asked the other man.

"To the Three Pigeons," answered Jared, ignoring the first question. On an impulse he put his hand in his pocket and drew out the nicked louis d'or.

"What's that?" asked the nearer man, thrusting the muzzle of his pistol into Jared's side.

"See for yourself," Jared answered.

The man gripped the coin, held it close to his face, fingered it, and passed it over to his companion, who repeated the performance.

"Aye," said the second man, and gave the gold-piece back to Jared. "We'll take them to the Captain," he announced. "One of us to either side of them. Step along there."

Jared and Hatch obeyed, and so were marched out from the woods and down to the shore of the river.

There was a wide beach here, lit by a number of fires, around which could be seen groups of men. Boats were drawn up on the sand, and on the higher ground beyond the fires was a row of small buildings.

Passing the last of the fires, the two guards led the strangers up to one of these buildings, which resembled a fisherman's shed. The door stood open, and there was a light inside. With a gruff, "We've brought two men to see you, Cap'n," Jared and Hatch were pushed over the threshold.

A ship's lantern, smelling strongly of oil, stood on a packing-case, and in a camp-chair close to it sat a man reading a tattered book that had lost its binding. The man looked up from his page, and, his eyes encountering the strangers, he gave a nod.

The reader was Norroy.

"We found them at the edge of the wood, Cap'n," said one of the men. "This fellow had the gold-piece," he added, pointing to Jared.

"Yes," said Norroy, laying the book on the packing-case and cocking one leg over the other. "You did well to bring them to me. I'll question them alone."

The men went out, and for a long moment Norroy sat motionless, his eyes on Jared's face.

"This is no place for a student of law, Master Lee," he said. "I told you to throw the louis d'or through the window."

"It has helped me twice now, once at the Three Pigeons and again in the woods," answered Jared.

"You received my letter?"

"Yes. I looked for you at the Three Pigeons last night. I saw Skipworth through the window."

"I've not been able to deal with him yet," said Norroy. "I regret that, I assure you, quite as much as you do. But I shall presently."

"The Marquis and his daughter are lost," said Jared. "They left Bellevue in Mellish's coach, but instead of being driven to Philadelphia they were driven south. They haven't been seen since."

"Ah!" exclaimed Norroy. "So that's the reason you are here."

"I remembered what you said about Skipworth, and your letter spoke of meeting him at the Three Pigeons and one of Mellish's men thought he had gone there."

"Excellently reasoned, oh student of law!" smiled Norroy. "I think from your statement of the case that we may conclude that Skipworth is somewhere in the south country."

"He certainly was last night. But, Hal, what I want to know is where to find Mademoiselle Jeanne and her father. And what are you doing here?"

Norroy looked at the tip of his boot. "I don't know where to find them. But I'll try to help you, Jared; and I have some influence in this neighborhood."

"What are you doing here? Why did those men call you Captain?"

Norroy glanced up with his quizzical smile. "I command a ship. You didn't know that was one of my accomplishments, did you? I am here because my ship lies offshore, and these men are part of her crew."

Jared stared at his friend. "Your crew? I don't understand. You're trying to mystify me."

"The situation is a somewhat peculiar one, I grant," said Norroy. "I don't wonder that it puzzles you. And yet it is simple enough. As I said before, I command a ship. I have spent many of my leisure hours studying navigation."

"I don't understand what you're doing here, Hal," Jared repeated. "We thought we'd fallen in with law-breakers; we were told not to prowl about this part of the shore; and yet here you are—the captain of a ship."

"Precisely. You state the situation with most commendable clearness. However, my presence here, and my ship and her crew, are not important to you, Jared. What you want is to find the French gentleman and his daughter and Cornelius Skipworth. I am with you in that, but circumstances compel me to postpone assisting you for a day or two."

"A day or two! But suppose they come to harm in the meantime?"

Norroy bit his lip while he considered that question. "You planned to go back to the Three Pigeons for the night, did you?"

"We did, but, Hal, if you can help us, why not at once?"

"I'll see what can be done. Believe me, Jared, I want to help you. This comes at an awkward time. You and your friend go to the Three Pigeons—I'll send a man with you to see you safe to the road— stay the night there, and I'll try to see you in the morning. If any one tries to make trouble for you show them the goldpiece and say the Captain gave it to you. The innkeeper is a rascal, but he'll keep his hands off any friend of mine. Yes, go now to the tavern." Norroy stood up, stepped to the door, and called out a name.

A man came up. "Sloat, you will take these two friends of mine to the highroad," ordered Norroy. "If any one interferes with their leaving camp report him to me." Turning, he put his hand on Jared's shoulder. "Don't puzzle your wits about me; I sha'n't forget your errand here; and I think I see a way to help you. Now go." And with a push he directed Jared to the door.

The light from the ship's lantern splashed outside on the ground. Overhead the clouds had broken away somewhat, letting enough light through to show the river and on its surface the outline of a ship. On the shore the camp-fires were ruddy splotches, with dark figures moving about them. To Jared it seemed a strange, mysterious scene, belonging to another world from anything he knew.

Hatch and he, accompanied by their guide, were now crossing the sand between the fires and the water. No one stopped them or called out to them. Jared glanced at Sloat. The look of the man told him nothing. He wanted to question this member of Norroy's crew, but prudence bade him hold his tongue.

They arrived at the woods and the guide was searching the trees for the entrance to the path when a sharp sound broke the night silence. A shot had been fired from the ship. Jared turned, and as he looked out over the water he saw a light flame from the bow. At the same instant Sloat gave an exclamation. "Here's your road! Be off with you!" he cried.

Without more words he ran across the high

ground to the beach. The camp was in motion. Men were leaving the fires and hurrying to the boats.

"It's a signal of some sort," said Hatch. "They're going aboard the ship."

"And Norroy?" said Jared. "Is he going too? He told us he was the captain." Suddenly a recollection flashed across his mind. "What was it that man at the inn and Skipworth were saying? They were plotting against the captain, they were going to do him some harm."

"Aye," agreed Hatch. "So I understood them."

Moved by a common impulse, the two went down the slope. Ahead, on the river, lay the ship, lights at her bow and stern. On the beach men were busy, pushing boats over the sand.

"We must find Norroy!" muttered Jared, and regardless of everything but the need of warning his friend, he broke into a run.

Some of the boats were in the water and men were climbing into them.

Looking for the tall figure of him who had declared himself the captain of this crew, Jared and Hatch raced along the shore, in and out between the boats.

"Hal! Norroy! Captain Norroy!" Jared cried. "Where is Captain Norroy?"

A man swore at him; another jeered in a loud voice.

Jared ran up to a boat that was afloat, and splashed into the water around it. The crew were shipping their oars. "Where is the Captain?" he called out.

"On his way aboard," someone answered. "That's his boat over there."

A brawny arm shot out and a hand seized Jared by the collar of his coat. "On board with you," roared a voice, "if you want to talk to the Cap'n!"

Another arm caught him around the waist and he was slung over the gunwale. He sprawled against knees and feet as the oars, dropping into the water, sent the boat away from the shore.

Not, however, before Hatch, at the stern, had leaped aboard and toppled a man from his seat by the impact of his heavy bulk. The man righted himself, swearing at Hatch's clumsiness. The crew, paying no attention to the altercation, bent to their oars and sent the boat leaping toward the ship.

XVIII

ABOARD THE SCHOONER

WHETHER they took him for a new member of the crew or for some fool who had come blundering among them, Jared did not know, nor did he have much opportunity to consider, for the distance from the shore to the ship was not far and the longboat had no more than brought up against the side of the larger vessel when one of the sailors prodded him in the back and he had to set foot on the rope-ladder and climb quickly aboard.

The crew of the longboat swarmed up after him and scattered over the deck. "Well, Master Lee," said Hatch at his elbow, "we're in for a sail. What do you make of it?"

"I'm sorry I got you into this," said Jared. "It's none of your affair."

"Don't you worry about me. I didn't have to come, but I'm blest if I'd stay ashore with you aboard."

The men on deck were too busy to notice them. Sails were being raised, an anchor chain creaked, orders were shouted fore and aft, boats were swung over the side. The schooner, under her mainsail, began to pick up the wind and draw away from the shore. Then Jared saw a tall figure approaching where Hatch and he stood in the shadow of the bulwark.

"Hal!" he exclaimed, stepping forward.

The other stopped and stared at Jared and his companion. "You here!" said Norroy. "Jared, why didn't you go?"

"I had something to tell you," answered Jared. "Some of your men mean you harm."

"I'd have had you keep out of this," said Norroy in a bitter voice. "Oh, you young fool!"

"We overheard talk last night at the Three Pigeons," said Jared.

Norroy made an impatient gesture. "Never mind the talk you heard! You're here, and I can't put you ashore. Come with me to my cabin."

The two followed him astern and descended to the cabin, where, after bolting the door, he bade them sit down. "Are you armed?" he demanded.

"Yes," said Jared, taking Kitt's pistol from his coat. "Both of us are armed."

Norroy sat down in front of the two and regarded them in silence for a moment.

" 'Tis the will of the gods, I suppose," he said; "but I never thought it possible you would set foot on this craft, Jared Lee. I don't know which is the bigger fool, you or I. But both of us, it seems, must swallow our folly. Now what is this tale you came to tell me?"

Jared related what he had heard outside the window of the Three Pigeons.

"And did you learn the name of Skipworth's companion?" Norroy asked when Jared had finished.

"Rand, I think it was."

Norroy nodded. "Rand is the mate. So he means to wait until after the brig is captured?" And he fell to thinking, a crease between his brows.

Presently he threw out an arm. "Doubtless I seem ungrateful when I ought to thank you, Jared, and your friend here. Had the tables been turned I should have acted as you did. But there is a vast difference in our positions. You respect the law, and I delight to break it. I have never let slip an opportunity to flout it when I could."

Silence filled the cabin while Jared looked at his friend, whose eyes were fixed upon him.

"I've always wondered about you," said Jared.

"But never understood me," returned Norroy. "No, and I don't think you ever will." He shifted in his seat, and for a moment looked down at his hand, which pressed against his thigh. "And since that is the case, we'd best not discuss it. I am, it seems, to be left in command of this ship until after the brig is captured. I have to take you with me;

though against your will, of course; but to Rand and the crew you must be one of us."

For the first time Hatch spoke up. "We might say we were recruited for your service, sir, by some of these men who are always looking for likely sailors. I've had them talk to me, trying to get me to give up farming for a taste of the sea. 'Twould be reasonable for your crew to consider us green hands."

"Possibly," said Norroy dryly. "No doubt you'd both prove green enough to justify such a story. No, I prefer to take Jared as ship's clerk, and you as an extra hand, under my orders. I'll explain this to Rand." He nodded, as if he had the situation settled to his liking. "Now I'll show you your quarters."

Near his own cabin was a spare room, roughly partitioned off from the after-part of the main hold, and fitted with three berths. Here Norroy left them, giving them good-night.

"Well, it might be worse," said the philosophic Hatch, when Jared and he were alone. "If this was the fo'c's'le now, like as not we'd be in hot water."

"This brig they talk of—" mused Jared. "As I understand it, Norroy's men plan to capture her."

"Aye, sir, that's about it. We've shipped aboard one of these craft that flies any flag it has a mind to, or no flag at all. I've heard tell of them, but I didn't think I'd ever ship aboard one. 'Tis like to be a strange adventure for a peaceable man."

The schooner went on her way, and the two who had so unexpectedly embarked on her cruise slept through the night. Next morning Jared and Hatch breakfasted in the main cabin with Norroy, who paid scant attention to them, however, but talked about the weather with the second mate, a lean, grizzled man by the name of Roach.

They were to be free of the ship, Norroy told them as he left the cabin, and when their appetites were appeased the two went on deck. The schooner was scudding southward under mainsail, topsail and jibs. There was no land in sight, only the wide, green water, shading to ultramarine, and the sky, cloud-billowed, through which shot rays of sunlight.

Forward on the deck they saw Rand, in peajacket and blue trousers, talking to one of the crew. Other men lounged amidships, and some of these eyed the strangers and seemed to whisper about them. Jared walked to the rail and rested his elbows on the heavy timber. Hatch came up beside him. "We're outside the Capes," he said. " 'Tis the Atlantic Ocean we're skimming over, my lad."

"I've always wanted to go to sea," said Jared. "I've talked about it with Simon Duckett, a ship chandler who sailed under Captain Paul Jones."

16

"And now you're here, how do you feel?" asked Hatch.

"Fit as a fiddle, Luke. I've got my sea-legs on."

Hatch nodded his approval. "Now this Captain Paul Jones; I know he was a great sailor, but he did some privateering too, seems to me I've heard."

"He fought the English," answered Jared. "Duckett says there's something about the sea that makes for lawlessness. He thinks that sailors have different views of right and wrong from landsmen. But Paul Jones—well, he may have been a privateer in wartime, but he never was a pirate."

"A word that's better not spoken where we be," cautioned Hatch. "Privateer sounds more friendly, and there's a war these days between the French and English. We're flying the French flag."

"But this brig they talk about is an American ship," Jared objected, "with a cargo from Philadelphia."

"Consigned to England perhaps?" Hatch suggested. "I've heard tell of the right of search."

"You argue like the Devil's advocate, Luke. You don't really think there's anything lawful about it."

Hatch gave a sheepish grin. "I know little enough about the law, master, but I've always heard as how a clever lawyer could make black look white."

"It would take a wonderfully clever lawyer to make this ship's business look anything but thievery to me!" retorted Jared. "How did Norroy ever come to it?"

"There's the love of danger and excitement and getting your hands on gold."

"Can't a man find those without turning outlaw?"

Hatch let his eyes brood on the green water. "Some get a warp in them when they're young; it's like a tree that's twisted early and never grows straight. It may be as strong as the other trees and as fit to bear good fruit, but it never does. I've known lads like that; something happened in their boyhood."

"I think that must have been the case with Norroy," Jared nodded. "Something made him a rebel. He grew up wild and uncared for, and he had some experience that set him against other men. But in spite of all this—" He struck the timber with his fist to emphasize his statement; "—in spite of this I think there's still something fine about him. He's not like Skipworth."

"I don't know as I ever blamed a tree for being twisted," Hatch said thoughtfully. "But I hate a mean fighter."

There was a movement of men on the deck amidships, and turning, the two saw a sail far to the westward. "The brig?" queried Hatch. "Are we going to chase her?"

Men gathered at the rail, pointing and gesticulating. They were a motley lot, dressed according to individual taste, and few of them wearing the usual sailor's garb, with which Jared had become familiar on the waterfront of Philadelphia. He judged they represented a number of races, he heard one man speaking French, and another a lingo that was unknown to him. Some were broad-shouldered and fair-skinned, while others were small and dark and full of gestures, like the Latin peoples.

Norroy appeared, and studied the distant sail through a glass. He spoke with Rand, and shortly word went about that the ship to the west was not the one they wanted. The crew scattered again, and the helmsman, at a command from the mate, changed the course of the schooner two points to the north.

Through that long summer day the ship, like a great winged bird, patrolled the ocean that lay outside the Capes of the Delaware. Ships were sighted and followed and abandoned. Toward sunset the wind dropped, the sails flattened and hung flapping. Sea and sky took on a roseate glow, and the schooner lifted over long, oily, opalescent rollers and slid down on the other side.

Jared and Hatch kept much to themselves, though now and then a sailor, passing their neighborhood, stopped for a word or two. They found there was an easy familiarity of the ocean, the sharing of a common deck brought tolerance at least. The mate

Rand, alone of the men, seemed to regard them with an inquisitive eye, but as he never spoke to them, either abovedeck or in the main cabin, they had no way of judging his thoughts.

Norroy kept aloof, only nodding when he met them at meal-times. To Jared he presented an altogether different appearance from that he had shown on shore. Gone was his lightsome humor and the twinkle of his eye. He was withdrawn both in look and manner, and when he spoke it was with a sharp, metallic ring, the note of authority.

Night rode on the sea, a night of stars and a gentle breeze that barely stirred the sails. The ship was like a gull, floating on the surface of undulating water, resting its wings until a wind should lift it in flight. Long Jared and Hatch sat on deck. When they went to their cabin Hatch said, "It must be a very difficult thing to pick up one special ship in such a might of water. Maybe the brig will get away and none here be any the wiser."

On the morrow the wind had risen again. Norroy changed the course. Sails were sighted, and like a hawk the schooner bore down upon them. Even to Jared's inexperienced eye it was evident that the ship could outsail any that she followed and that the captain and crew knew how to make the most of her swiftness. And yet time and again as the sun that day ascended to the meridian he echoed

Hatch's thought: In such a might of water the brig might well get away without their having seen her.

At dinner in the main cabin a sailor brought a message to Norroy and he went on deck. Those below heard orders shouted and a scuffling of feet. The ship stirred and shivered; she was headed on a new tack. As Jared put his head above the companionway he saw another ship, two-masted and square-rigged, bearing off to the south.

A sailor pointed. "Yon's our brig!" he cried, "and a time we've had to find her!"

There seemed to be no misdoubt. There was a wild excitement in every man on deck that Jared hadn't noticed before. With every inch of canvas drawing the schooner swooped on and on, throwing great crests of water to the rigging from her sharp prow.

The brig, as though she had sensed something unfriendly in the white wings bearing down on her, commenced to fetch more and more to the east. The schooner copied her tactics, sheering off, but maintained her great pace. For a time the course lay so, the pursuer gaining a little with every shift of the wheel. Then through the ripping turmoil of flying water Norroy barked an order and a gun thundered from the schooner's bow.

A splash in the water on the port side of the brig, and a geyser rose in the air. The schooner shook with the recoil of the gun, but lost not a second's headway.

Jared was now at the rail, watching the other ship, which seemed to him like a live thing, frightened by a hunter and not knowing where to turn. He could see the crew on her deck, running hither and yon in obedience to commands. But in spite of her straining canvas she was fast being overhauled.

The schooner swooped on, assured, magnificent, tearing through scudding seas, her great beak cleaving the water and tossing it to either side. A second shot sped from her gun and plumped into the wake at the stern of the brig. There was a cheer from the schooner's crew. "The next tears a hole in your side!" Jared heard a deep voice roar.

The brig, flustered, with her enemy at her heels, and the next shot likely to rip the masts from her deck, fell off, as if in mind to try another tack. The maneuver was useless, however. With the slackening of the brig's speed the schooner darted forward, and with a rush was upon her. Close to the brig's side she swung, sheered off, and with a rattling of blocks dropped some of her canvas. Norroy gave an order and grappling-irons were thrown out. The schooner's gun was levelled at the brig. Muskets and pistols were thrust over the rail of the captor.

The captain of the brig ran up a white flag.

Norroy's answer was a command for him to come aboard the schooner with his chief officer.

The command was quickly obeyed, and Norroy and Rand conducted the two men from the brig to the schooner's cabin, while Roach, the cannon loaded, stood ready on deck to overpower any attempt at opposition on the part of the brig's crew.

XIX

THE FIGHT IN THE CABIN

THE talk in the cabin must have been much to the point, for within ten minutes Norroy and Rand and the two men from the brig reappeared on deck. The captain of the brig remained as a hostage for the good behavior of his men, while his chief officer, with Rand and a dozen of the schooner's crew, went aboard the other ship. Then began a carrying of boxes and bales and barrels from the hold of the brig to her deck, the swinging of them up over the side of the schooner, and the depositing of them on board.

Jared and Hatch watched these proceedings from a distance, each hotly indignant at this treatment of a peaceful merchantman. There had been a thrill to the chase, a sense of reckless excitement; but this they now witnessed was simply thievery—piracy in short.

Boxes followed bales and barrels until the most part of the brig's cargo was in the hold of the schooner. Jared heard the schooner's men declare that "this was a wonderful rich haul!" that "this was a great day's work!" His sympathy went out to the captain of the brig, who stood apart, watching with angry eye the despoiling of his ship.

An hour was needed for the transfer, and then, the brig's commander having been put aboard his ship, the schooner stood away. As the water widened between them Jared's eyes brooded on the other vessel, which, with sails idly flapping, looked like a hapless derelict in the great waste of the sea.

He felt disgust at the business. There was no glamour to such a trade as this, only men who were more like wolves than human beings could engage in it. He thought of stories he had read of buccaneers and pirates, of men like Kidd and Blackbeard; they had thrilled him once; he had even felt a sneaking admiration for sea rovers when he had listened to Simon Duckett in his chandler's shop. He would feel neither the thrill nor the sneaking admiration again. If there had been a fight his sensation might have been different. But the capture of the brig had been simply the act of a bully who robs a defence-less child.

And Norroy, his friend and once on a time his pattern! Norroy, who was the captain of this schooner and the leader of these wolves! Jared shrugged his shoulders. There were indeed in this world things past his understanding. If any one had told him a week ago that Norroy was a black-hearted villain Jared would have said that he lied.

He went below deck, and as he passed the door of the captain's cabin he saw Norroy standing there, studying a paper outspread on a shelf. Norroy turned, and their glances met. A message flashed in Norroy's, and Jared stepped into the cabin.

"Shut the door," said Norroy.

Jared obeyed, and stood with his back to the door.

He felt that he was looking at a man he had known, but only partly recognized now. There was no lift to the shoulders or the head, no gaiety in the eyes. Instead the mouth was tightened at the corners, and the eyes were lack-lustre; there were seams in the cheeks that had been so full.

"A sorry piece of business, eh?" said Norroy. "Yes, Jared, so it is." He tapped the outspread paper with his finger. "I wish the brig's cargo were sunk in the bottom of the sea!"

For a space there was silence between them. Jared, his back against the door, stood looking at this man who, once so debonair and fascinating, now appeared grim and morose. After a time Norroy stepped over to a cupboard and took out a bottle of brandy and a glass. He drank a stiff potion, and returned the glass and bottle. "Jared," he said turning, "I'm through with it!"

Jared nodded.

"You haven't forgotten what I told you about the mate and Skipworth?" he asked.

"No, not I." Norroy took a few paces up and down the cabin. "Nor have I forgotten the errand that brought you from Philadelphia. Once ashore that shall be my chief concern." His brow lightened a little, and he added, "Maybe I can do somewhat to take the taste of this out of my mouth before we part company."

That was all that was said between them. Jared opened the door and went out into the passage. In his own cabin he lay down on a berth and fell into a slumber which lasted until Hatch shook his arm and told him the cook was serving supper.

Rand was in the main cabin when they entered, and so was Norroy. The latter was talking about the cargo they had taken from the brig; it was a rich haul, and should bring a good price in the West Indies, where they intended to sell it. He seemed to be in high spirits over the successful outcome of their venture. Rand, who was never very talkative, listened, and said a few words, chiefly contemptuous references to the craven nature of merchant ship commanders.

When the mate had finished and withdrawn on deck Norroy lighted a pipe and, pushing his chair back from the head of the table, stretched his legs at ease. At the foot of the table sat Jared and Hatch, on opposite sides. A lamp, hanging from the ceiling, swung above their heads with the motion of the ship.

Hatch made a movement to rise, but Norroy detained him with a gesture. "Master Lee tells me you're a fighting man," he said. "I used to know a number of good fighting men when I was in England."

"Aye, I can use my fists," Hatch made answer. "And, begging your pardon, sir, I think it a better trade than what some follow at sea."

"I knew one fighting man," Norroy continued suavely, "who was sent to jail for ten years because he broke the head of a nobleman who insulted his sweetheart. The man had been a groom in my father's stables. A pretty matter this business of justice, when you see how it works."

"That's the fault of having privileged classes," put in Jared. "A nobleman against a groom."

"Yes," said Norroy, and drew on his pipe for a few minutes in silence. "Yet I knew one of the privileged classes who had to choose between going to prison and flying from England because he helped a poor devil of a thief out of a tight hole. If the thief had been captured, he'd have been hung. That's the law of England."

"But this man you knew, this nobleman," said Jared, "could have used his influence at the king's court to help him out, couldn't he?"

Norroy shook his head. "He didn't have a very good account to render to those who sat in high places, Jared. He'd preferred the society of low-born rogues to that of rascally peers of the realm, you see."

Thereupon he laid his pipe on the table and dropped one hand to his knee, twisting his head slightly as if he were listening to some sound that had just caught his attention.

Next minute a big bulk stood in the door of the cabin, and Jared turned to see the swarthy, truculent face of Rand.

"I want a private word with you, Captain," said the mate, walking toward the table.

"Very good," said Norroy. "But if it's to be in private, what are those two men doing there behind you?"

"They're to take charge of these fellows," declared the mate, pointing at Jared and Hatch. "The crew don't know anything about them, and want to know more before we go ashore."

"That's right," muttered one of the two men who had entered in the wake of Rand and now stood between him and the door.

"I vouch for them," said Norroy shortly. "That's enough for you to know."

"It was, up to now." The mate's voice had an aggressive, ugly note. "But before this ship comes to land we want to make certain they won't inform against us."

"So?" said Norroy. "And isn't my word sufficient for you and the crew? I'll talk to you, Rand; but not till those two men get out of the cabin."

"No," answered the mate. "They don't go without your friends. That's what the crew have decided."

"The crew—decided?" echoed Norroy. He raised his right hand from his lap and set his fist on the table and in it there was gripped a pistol, cocked and pointed.

"Now!" he said, and his eyes glinted like two sharp bits of steel.

One of the men behind the mate brought his hand around from his back. In the same second Jared leaped from his chair, swinging his arm downward.

There was a loud report, and a bullet sped across the table, deflected in its aim by a scant inch or two.

The pistol that Norroy held, struck in the barrel, was torn away from his hand.

Hatch sprang to his feet; so did Norroy. Jared, who was nearest to Rand, turned on him like a flash.

The next moment Jared had seized the mate around the knees, and with a mighty heave of back and shoulders sent him crashing to the floor. The man who had fired the shot that began the business leaped at Jared, aiming a blow at his head with the stock of the pistol; but Hatch fetched him a blow with his fist on the side of the jaw that stretched him full-length, like a tree struck by lightning.

The cabin shook with the racket. Norroy, hearing the mate's curses as Jared brought him to the floor, had sprung at the third man and wrenched his pistol from him, and his voice now rang out, "Get back there, you, get back!" as he drove him aft of the cabin.

Jared stood up from the mate. "Out of here, both of you, Jared and Hatch!" ordered Norroy, and with a final lunge at the man in front of him that brought him against the wall at the farther end of the cabin, he turned and ran after them to the open door.

Up the companionway was blue sky, brilliant with the glow of the late summer sunset, and on the deck was the sound of feet, men hurrying to see what had happened.

Norroy shut the cabin door behind him. "Hatch, you have a pistol," he said. "Stand here, and if any of those three open that door a crack put a bullet in him." Then, with the pistol he had wrenched from the third man in his hand, he sprang up the stairs, Jared at his heels.

Faces were staring as he leaped on deck, and it flashed through Jared's mind that if Rand had actually spoken for the crew when he told of their supposed decision Norroy and he were likely to have short shrift meted them now.

The men, however, fell back before the captain as he swept his eyes around them. "Where's Roach?" he said, and, as the second mate stepped up, he continued, "I have three men in the cabin who deserve to hang."

Then, with pistol gripped in hand, he said in a voice that bit like ice, "I'm the captain of this ship, and if any man dares to question that, I'll deal with him as I have with those three wretches!"

The crew was a hard-visaged lot, but none of them spoke a word. And Jared, looking from face to face, realized that even among pirates there was a sharp line set between master and man.

"Roach," said Norroy, "you will have the carpenter nail up the door of the main cabin. You understand me, men?" he said, again addressing the crew. "Then get back to your stations."

The men scurried away. "Roach," said Norroy, "this has been a bad day's work for Rand. But for you there will be a share of what would have come to him from the brig's cargo."

With that Norroy, turning, hooked his left arm through the right arm of Jared, and, with the pistol swinging down against his leg, walked forward on the deck.

XX

INDIAN RIVER BAY

MUTINY, if mutiny there had been in the minds of the schooner's crew, seemed to have vanished with the outcome of the fight in the cabin. Jared was inclined to the opinion that the plan had been concocted by Rand and his two companions and not yet divulged to any of the others; and that the mate had intended, when he had disposed of Norroy, to assume command of the ship by virtue of his office and the fear he could instil in the men.

"They are easily led, Jared," Norroy said, as the two walked the deck. "Men want to be led. All they require, whether they enlist in the service of the saints or the devil, is someone to point them the way and give them a watchword. The history of the world has been made by a comparatively small number of men; most of the inhabitants of this revolving sphere have been much like this ship's crew, inarticulate, slow-witted and huddled together, and moving, when they do move, only because some forceful individual has imposed his will on them."

That his men knew their captain was such an individual, one neither to be frightened nor thwarted, Jared could well believe as the schooner, without any further commotion, plowed her way westward through the summer night. Hatch joined Norroy on deck, telling him that the carpenter had made fast the main cabin door.

Roach appeared, and was given his instructions. Norroy would keep the deck for the night, and Jared and Hatch would divide the watches with him.

It was shortly after dawn next morning, and Jared had just disposed of a steaming cup of coffee in the galley, when land was sighted to the southwest. For several hours the schooner held her course, and then bore more to the southward. "This should bring us," Hatch said to Jared at the rail, "round the point of Delaware and a score of miles below Lewes. There are wide bays there and many little rivers."

That it was not Norroy's purpose to bring the schooner back to the anchorage from which she had sailed was soon evident. He disclosed something of his plan when he presently spoke to Jared. "We unload our cargo in Indian River Bay and store it there until a ship clears for the West Indies. And there it may be we will find our friend Skipworth and give him a chance to speak his mind to me, as he vowed to Rand he would."

"Why should he be there?" asked Jared.

"Because he's a clerkly individual and likes to keep a check-list of all the cargoes that are brought

in from these trips at sea. He makes his percentage
of them in return for the information he supplies."

"So that is his business," said Jared.

Norroy's eye twinkled in the old familiar way.
"One of them, my boy. He has several. I know
of an occasion when he took the Chester Road and
nearly made off with the roan of a young man who
was riding to Philadelphia."

"That highwayman was Skipworth!"

Norroy nodded. "He meant to pay you back for
the blow you gave him at Bellevue. But that was
a low-down act of treachery on the part of Cornelius.
There was an unwritten law that none of Joshua
Mellish's guests were to be molested, and in addition he knew that you were a friend of mine."

"I never thought the robber was Skipworth."

"The notion popped into my head that night,"
went on Norroy, "that he might try such a game;
that was what brought me back at a gallop. It was
hard to resist the temptation to use my pistol on
him. But I scored it to his account. And now,
since you've brought me the tale of his talk with
Rand at the Three Pigeons, the reckoning with him
is due. What was the name he called me?"

"As I remember he said you were too much of
a parson."

"A parson, yes." Norroy clasped his hands behind his back and stared out over the sea. "Coming from him that might be regarded as a compliment. But I'm afraid the good Cornelius is not very familiar with gentlemen of the cloth."

"And Mademoiselle Jeanne?" asked Jared.

Norroy turned his head and looked into the eyes of the young fellow who stood beside him. "Yes. What business have I to think of my own affairs when there is any question of what has befallen that innocent lady? But I tell you this. When I have Skipworth before me he shall tell us where she is if I have to whip the answer from him! He'll speak, the dog!"

Nearer and nearer to the coast the schooner bore over the ocean. Sails were far away to the north, but none to the west or south, for the ship was now outside the routes of sea-borne traffic. The shore was continually indented, and seemingly as untouched by man's hand as in the days when the first explorers set eyes upon its woods.

So light was the breeze that afternoon that it was not until after sunset that the schooner threaded her way through a network of low-lying reefs and dropped her anchor in a wide bay. This land-locked expanse of water, now a mirror of gold with scarcely a ripple on its surface, was so quiet and still that the plunge of the anchor, breaking the hush of twilight, sent a score of birds wheeling across the shore.

There was a sandy beach and at the western end of it the mouth of a small river, which was lost in trees. At the junction of beach and estuary was a wooden building, which Jared took to be the place where the schooner stored her cargoes. He saw several men on the sand, who waved to the ship's crew and exchanged greetings with them. Meantime the schooner's sails were lowered and furled under the direction of Roach.

A word from Norroy on the forward deck brought Jared and Hatch to him. "I've been puzzling over the situation," he said, "and what I make out of it is this: Skipworth may not be among the men on shore, but if he isn't in the neighborhood he will be here soon. It would be better if he didn't find you two in my company. And, looking at it from another angle, I should feel easier with you off the ship. The crew may begin to ask questions, and the better course I've always found is to act first and explain afterwards. Therefore, I'm going to set you ashore with a bag of provisions. Once ashore, I'll tell you what to do."

A boat was dropped alongside, and Norroy ordered four men into it. Jared and Hatch, each with a bag containing a small store of food slung over his shoulder, took their places in the boat, with

Norroy in the sternsheets. A short row brought them to the beach, where Norroy directed his crew to wait for him, while he and Jared and Hatch walked up on the sand.

Norroy started toward the building at the mouth of the river, but when he was well away from the eyes of the men in the boat he turned toward the woods which ran along the edge of the beach. In the shelter of the trees he stopped. "I'm not going to bid you goodby, Jared," he said. "I want you both where I can find you when I need you. But until Skipworth comes you are better out of sight. My men keep to the bay and rarely go into the country. Through these woods to the north you will come to another beach, not a quarter-mile distant. There you can lie snug. No one will molest you. The schooner will stay at anchor until another ship arrives to take her cargo aboard, and meantime we will have Master Skipworth where we can interrogate him."

With that he stepped a little farther into the woods. "Hatch," said he, "are you as good a forrester as you are a fighter?"

"I can find my way if you start me in the right direction," was the confident answer.

"There then, to the north. A hundred yards and you can see the water."

Hatch set out, with Jared back of him, and

through the woods they made their way to an open upland and down to a second beach.

This was hidden from the schooner by a long finger of land which ran out into the ocean. The stars showed only the sand, groves in the distance, and the phosphorescent sheen of the land-encircled bay. There was no glimpse of house or tilled field; only the rustle and whirr of some surprised bird broke the night silence.

"Ever camped out, Master Lee?" asked Hatch.

"Often," answered Jared.

"This is better than yon ship," said Hatch. "I've had my fill of sailing. I'll sleep sounder on a bed of moss than in that schooner's cabin, wondering how soon it'll be before someone points a pistol at me."

"Yes," agreed Jared, "we're well out of that. But, Luke, we've lost time in our hunt for the Marquis and his daughter."

"We'll come up with them, master. We're certain to. And it won't be many more days, neither."

They chose a camp ground at the edge of a grove, where a slope of moss provided a soft bed. There were no doubts here to assail them, none of that constant sense of possible peril that had been with them when they lay down to sleep on the schooner. The night was warm, and the lap of water on the shingle lulling to their ears. Jared, making a pillow of fragrant pine branches, was soon asleep.

When he woke a sheet of glinting, orange-hued water shone in his eyes, the sun was above the sea-line. Birds were twittering in the grove behind his head. He lay still for a few moments, then moved his limbs gently, rubbing the kinks from them. He sat up, and the motion wakened Hatch, who looked at him out of one sleepy eye.

"I'm going to take a swim," said Jared, pulling off his coat.

"As you say, Master Lee. I'll take a few more winks."

Hatch turned over, sheltering his eyes from the gleaming bay. Jared piled his clothes in a heap, and ran over the sand to the water.

The first taste of it was cold, but deliciously stirring. An excellent swimmer, he struck out with delight toward the headland to the north.

Used as he was to swimming in an inland river, this experience of salt water was uncommonly exhilarating. He had the sensation of having the world to himself, a world of clear, cool water, with fresh green verdure to bound it and a cloudless, sun-filled sky overhead. Turning after a while toward the point where an ochre line of sand dunes, topped by straggling bushes, formed one end of the arc of the bay he found he could touch bottom, and walked shoreward, splashed through the shallower water, and ran up on the beach.

The sun felt good on his wet skin, and throwing himself on the sand he rolled over on it, like a puppy at play. Warm again, he sat up and looked about him. Not far on his left hand was the tip of the headland. He felt the desire to explore.

At a jog-trot he pattered over the sand to the point that made the northern extremity of the crescent. As he had supposed, the ocean beyond flowed inland, the shoreline here being a succession of curves. But what at once caught his eye, as soon as he had rounded the last sand dune, was the figure of a man who had just landed from a skiff with a string of fish in his hand.

Jared dropped to his knees, for the man was not thirty yards away from him, and he had no desire to be seen. A clump of thorn bushes provided him with a sufficient screen, behind which he might raise his head and observe the stranger.

The man pulled his skiff up on the beach, out of reach of the tide, and picked up the string of fish. As he did this he turned, and Jared instantly recognized him as the man in brown.

Jacques Latour here! What did that mean?

The Frenchman, who was without coat or hat, and whose sleeves were rolled up to the shoulder, swung the line of fish in his hand and walked off along the beach in the opposite direction from the headland where Jared was crouching.

Following him with his eyes, Jared saw that above this next scallop of shore lay a grassy meadow and beyond that in a grove of trees was the partly revealed outline of a house. Latour presently left the beach and went toward this building.

Jared turned and ran back over the sand to the place where Hatch and he had camped. Luke was munching bread and dried beef, and an uncorked water-bottle was propped against a bush beside him. "Didn't see any one, did you?" he asked, looking up at Jared with a grin, "to make you come back hot-foot instead of through the water?"

"I saw the Frenchman Latour. He landed around the point over there with a string of fish."

Hatch gave a whistle. "You don't tell me so!"

"He went up to a house above the beach," continued Jared. "What's he doing here, Luke? What do you make of that?"

Hatch took a bite from his loaf of bread. "Most like he's doing the same as what everyone seems to be doing in this part of the country, and that's something deceitful."

Dried by the warm sun, Jared put on his clothes, and proceeded to eat his breakfast. As he munched he talked. "I'm going to find out what Latour is doing. Norroy said there was no one along this shore but his own people. He must be mistaken about that. There's that house, and there's Latour ....Luke, why would any one bring the Marquis and his daughter down to this lonely country?"

"We don't know as how any one did, Master Lee."

"What's Latour doing here then?"

Brooding on that question, Jared finished his breakfast and jumped to his feet.

"I'm going to have a look at that house. I can reach it through the trees."

"And what about the schooner?" asked Hatch. "I don't want to lose sight of her. Suppose this Skipworth comes, and suppose he can outtalk the captain—for I don't trust that crew of his no further than I can see them—and they turn on him when he gets ashore; why, then, Master Lee, it might be I could put in a word or a blow that would be to Captain Norroy's advantage. And there's this other ship we've heard about that may come in any time. I want to know what's going on there." He nodded southward in the direction of the bay where the schooner had anchored.

"All right," said Jared. "You go that way, and I'll go this. We'll come back here to report what we learn."

"Don't you come to blows with that Frenchman," cautioned Hatch. "Like as not he's a rascally fighter."

With a nod, but without an answer—for Jared was now too intent on learning more about Latour to waste further words—he struck inland from their camp, having in mind to approach the house by a half-circle from the rear and so escape being seen.

XXI

WHAT JARED OVERHEARD

As JARED went up from the beach and crossed the meadow, the woods that fringed their camp shut off the breeze and the air was still and hot. The field was knee-deep in grass, through which in places shone the yellow of buttercups, and to one side was a pool of great white daisies. Dragonflies winged their zigzag course, small rainbow particles glittering in the sunlight. The new leaves of aspens and birches were light green clouds caught in the darker forest trees.

Turning from the meadow, Jared walked through the welcome shade of the woods to a second field, from which he had another view of the ocean, very high and wide. Stopping here, he studied the landscape. To the south he made out the ribbon of a road, which he supposed led from the nearest settlements of Indian River Bay. The house he was seeking must be somewhere near that road, so he turned in that direction. Traversing a field of clover, he came to a clump of pines and beyond this saw the silvery-gray boards of a fair-sized dwelling.

Between him and the house was a roughly-fenced-in enclosure, in which at the moment a sow and her

litter of small pigs were giving vent to a chorus of
loud, indignant grunts.   Beyond the pen a dozen
hens were picking at the short grass while a lordly
rooster, with magnificent iridescent green tail
feathers, was daintily lifting his feet in a stately
promenade.

The house had a shabby appearance.   Jared judged
that it had been built by some early settler, who
had thought to acquire for himself a comfortable
property from the surrounding land, and so had
constructed a dwelling that should suit his ambitious
needs.   From hand to hand it had passed, with little
done to it in the way of repair or improvement,
until it had fallen into the possession of some shiftless tenant, who had been content to have a roof
over his head and to make a living with as little
effort as he could.

A lilac bush stood at the back, and several small
rose trees, already in bloom, were between the house
and the road.   At the front was a small square
hedge of dark green box, which indicated that here
had once been a garden.   But the steps that led down
from the front porch were sagging and broken, and
the few evidences of a prosperous past only served
to accentuate its present uncared-for appearance.

Several windows were open on the side that fronted
toward Jared, but no one was to be seen   The pigs
grunted and the elegant rooster, having picked his

way to the road, executed a graceful about-face and returned to exhibit his beauty to the bevy of busy hens.

Jared was considering the advisability of stepping into the clearing when the back door of the house was pushed open and a woman came out. Immediately Jared drew back among the pines. The woman wore an old calico dress and carried a wooden pail. She went directly to the pig-pen and threw the refuse of her kitchen to the sow and litter.

The grunts changed to squeals of satisfaction. The woman emptied the pail and instantly half-a-dozen snouts immersed themselves in dinner. The rooster stalked over to have a look at the occasion of such excitement and eyed the uncouth beasts with a cold and haughty glare.

The provider of the meal muttered a few admonitions that Jared could not catch. Then she turned from the pen and walked back toward the house. Before she reached the steps, however, a man came out at the door. He was sallow-faced, lanky and raw-boned. He said something to the woman, and, as she went in, he slouched across to the road and disappeared to the south.

That these were the tenants of the place Jared did not doubt. And having seen them he could well understand why the house and its surroundings looked so unkempt. Shiftless and idle he presumed them to be, a couple who had lodged here by chance and who had made no effort whatever to repair what had originally been a fine country mansion.

Now, save for the munching of the pigs, the clearing was as quiet as the meadow that stretched in front of the house and the blue bay beyond it. Jared wondered what he should do. To go up to the door and seek to question the woman would expose him to the risk of meeting Latour, who would want to know what he was doing in this part of the country.

Debating the best course to follow, he took a few steps through the grove in the direction of the water, careful to keep himself out of sight of any one in the house. This brought him a view of the front door, and as he stopped the door opened and a man appeared. It was Latour, and he was speaking to someone back of him and beckoning.

Latour walked along the porch to the sagging, broken steps that led down to what had been the small, box-bordered garden. Out from the house, following Latour, came the Marquis de Severac, very tall and thin, his face in the full light the yellow-white of ivory.

The garden was only a few paces from the edge of the pines. Jared took a couple of steps backward, and saw, to his satisfaction, that Latour hadn't discovered him.

18

The Marquis went down the treacherous steps of the porch slowly and carefully and so came up with the vigorous young Frenchman. He drew a handkerchief from his coat and touched his forehead with it. Jared heard him say in French: "It seems an extremely warm morning, Latour."

And in French—a tongue which Jared thanked his stars he understood—Latour replied, "This America has not the agreeable climate of our own land, monsieur."

"Ah no, I think it has not." The Marquis, touching his handkerchief now to his cheeks and chin, regarded his fellow-countryman with uplifted eyebrows.

"We will remedy that, monsieur." Even at the distance at which he stood from the speaker Jared noted the insolence of his tone. "There will be a ship here at any moment that will bear monsieur and his daughter and me to the West Indies, and thence we will go to Havre. That is the reason why I asked for a few words with you out of mademoiselle's hearing—to lay my plans before you."

"No, Latour, we don't wish to return to Havre," said the Marquis.

The other man stuck his hands on his hips and thrust his head forward. Jared remembered that this fellow was the son of a notary in the Normandy village that had for centuries been a fief of the

Sieurs de Severac, and had led the mob that had attacked the château. Doubtless now in France he might be a man of importance in his native province.

This idea was also evidently uppermost in the mind of Latour. "I need hardly point out to you, monsieur," he observed, "that conditions have altered in our country. The king no longer rules there, and the nobles have lost their privileges. Liberty, equality and fraternity are now the watchwords of France."

The Marquis bent his head in acquiescence. "They are fine words, but I failed to find any of those ideals in the mob that despoiled my home. The liberty appears to be license, the equality and fraternity the right to take what doesn't belong to one."

"You misunderstand us, monsieur. The principle of the new order is that the peasant is as good as the tradesman and the tradesman as good as the Marquis. We are all brothers in fact. Latour is now on an equal footing with De Severac."

"So it seems," admitted the Marquis. "But I have lived so long under the old order that I find it difficult to accustom myself to the new."

"You would find it necessary to accustom yourself to it in France, and that very quickly."

The nobleman waved his hand. He appeared to assent to that proposition likewise.

"Look you now, monsieur," said Latour, "since

it seems you understand the situation. I, being of an equality with you, have the honor of asking for the hand of your daughter."

De Severac drew back a step, as if something vile had touched him. A faint flush came in the ivory-whiteness of his thin, bony face. "And I, Monsieur Latour," he answered, "have the—honor of declining your request."

The other man thrust out his hand. "That is your first impulse, but I ask you to reconsider. You have not yet grasped the complete meaning of our new equality."

"I comprehend it," said the Marquis. "But that makes no difference to me. If I should consider your suggestion from now until doomsday my answer would be the same."

"You are stubborn," Latour retorted; "but there are necks as stubborn as yours that have bowed to the blast in France. For mark you, when you and mademoiselle and I land at Havre it will not be Monsieur the Marquis de Severac, but Monsieur Jacques Latour, who will give the word of command."

"I have no intention of landing at Havre," said the nobleman.

"Ah, Monsieur, but I have the intention of seeing you landed there, you and your daughter. As I said a few moments ago the ship to convey us may be here today or tomorrow. There is no question about it. We are here in this solitary spot, and the ship is expected in the bay yonder. And when we arrive at Havre it may be that I, Latour, will be able to satisfy our compatriots concerning the Marquis, provided I announce myself as monsieur's son-in-law." He waited a moment to give effect to his words. "Monsieur will go with mademoiselle and me to the priest and bestow on us his blessing, or— he will go to prison. And in the latter event mademoiselle and I will be united without the pleasure of his blessing."

There was silence in the sunny square bordered by the ancient box hedge. The man of the old nobility stood like a wavering pine, buffeted by the rude breath of this new, self-assertive order.

"I have admired monsieur's daughter," Latour remarked in a more subdued tone, "ever since I can remember. Formerly it appeared that there was a gap between us. But when all Frenchmen were declared equal, any difference due to the mere accident of station disappeared. I took my resolve at once to make Mademoiselle Jeanne my wife. With that object I came to this country. I feel that I will be able to win her favorable regard when I come to speak with her. She is young, and perhaps sees things differently from you, monsieur."

"I can tell you how she will see this matter," said

the Marquis in a low voice. "She will understand you give us the choice between her consent and my imprisonment. On her behalf I make the choice; give me up to my enemies."

"Perhaps, however, monsieur's daughter will not feel that way. She may prefer to accept my proposal rather than have her father sacrifice himself."

The Marquis shrugged his high shoulders. He had evidently no wish for further argument.

"There is one other alternative, monsieur," continued Latour. "If Mademoiselle Jeanne wishes it I might procure a priest at the nearest village here to make us man and wife at once. In that case you need not sail to Havre with us. You could remain here in peace and security. It goes without my mentioning it that Madame Latour would be entirely safe with me in France."

"That alternative is as distasteful to me as the other," answered De Severac. "And again I speak for my daughter."

"I prefer that mademoiselle should speak for herself," declared Latour. "I have placed the situation before you. Now I shall feel free to discuss it with her."

The Marquis raised his hand, the handkerchief clutched in his fingers. But there was no profit in an insult; it would only make his situation more impossible. Tremblingly he turned, as if to shield his daughter from speech with the villain, and mounting the broken steps, crossed the porch and went in at the front door.

For a moment Latour, hands on his hips and his feet wide apart, stood looking after him. Then, with a muttered imprecation, he left the box-bordered garden and followed the Marquis into the house.

XXII

CORNELIUS SKIPWORTH

THE impulse to walk out from the pines and speak his mind to Latour, using if need be his fists or the pistol that was still in his coat pocket, had been strong upon Jared, and it was only the thought that such an intervention on his part might result in more injury than benefit to the cause of the Marquis and Jeanne that caused him to remain where he was. Latour might himself be armed, or have confederates in the house who would come to his aid; and if Jared should fail to settle the score with him then and there Latour would have the advantage of knowing that Jared was in the neighborhood and could take measures against him.

It was the fact that Latour was ignorant of the presence of friends of the Marquis that seemed to Jared to offer the best hope of a rescue. The Frenchman would presumably be looking for no interference in his plans; evidently he had come to some terms with the pirates who made Indian River Bay their base and from that harbor sent their stolen cargoes oversea to ports where their loot could be disposed of without awkward questions. With the aid of Mellish's villain of a coachman Latour had brought his prisoners down to this coast, where there was no one concerned at thwarting evil-doers, had probably paid the tenants of the house to keep them there and see that they didn't leave, and had arranged for passage for them on the ship that carried the pirates' booty. Norroy had said that the ship would sail to the West Indies, and Latour had said that he would take them thence to Havre. With De Severac and his daughter in Latour's possession the latter would doubtless be able to convey them securely to France.

That plan, as Jared had just overheard it propounded to the Marquis, made him hot and cold at one and the same time. There was a devilishness about it that exceeded anything Jared had ever heard. In France, as Jared knew from reports that had come from that country, the old nobility were being seized, thrown into prison, and even beheaded by an instrument called the guillotine. Such men as Jacques Latour were governing the country, and their slightest whim was law. It was easy to understand that, once in France, a word from Latour would send the Marquis to prison, and possibly to execution. That would leave Mademoiselle Jeanne at Latour's mercy, and such a man as he would be sure to drive his own bargain. It needed no thought on Jared's part to know that Jeanne would despise such a creature; but if she were confronted with the alternative of her father's execution or her own self-sacrifice what would she do? The answer to that question Jared thought he knew.

Latour might now be urging his suit upon her, and she, poor girl, be turning from him in disgust. But Jared swore to himself that the situation in which the villainous Frenchman was planning to place her—in which indeed he thought he already had her—should never actually come to pass. Jeanne should never set sail on that ship. He would find some way to prevent it. He was here, and so was Luke Hatch, and there was Norroy to help them.

All this he considered quickly. As he stood there, sizing up the situation, he saw the sallow-faced man who had gone out at the back door, return along the road and go into the house. He would, of course, take his orders from Latour. Yes, thought Jared, it was not the right time for him, single-handed, to attempt a rescue.

It took but a short time for Jared to regain the meadow and the half-moon bay where Hatch and he had camped. The place was deserted and quiet, except for the distant cries of terns and gulls that hung above the water, searching the shallows, until at the sight of a fish they dropped into the waves.

His first need was to find Hatch, and with that object in view Jared crossed the beach and went into the woods that sheltered it on the south.

This was the route Hatch and he had followed the night before, and without hesitation Jared directed his steps to the point where they had parted from Norroy. He reached the last trees and had the wide shore and gleaming water of Indian River Bay lying just beyond. But instead of one schooner there were now two ships in the bay; a second schooner was coming to anchor off the mouth of the river, a beautiful white-winged vessel that at any other time would have held Jared in rapt admiration.

This must be the ship that would take the pirates' loot to market, the ship that Jacques Latour purposed should carry Jeanne and her father to France.

Jared saw men on the beach around the storehouse and on the decks of the two schooners; and then he heard a rustle in the woods to his right and turned to discover Hatch treading softly among the trees.

"Yon's the ship they're waiting for," said Hatch in a low tone, pointing toward the schooner that lay off the entrance to the river. "I saw her come in an hour ago; and they're making ready to put a cargo aboard her."

"Luke," said Jared, "the Marquis and his daughter are prisoners of Latour in the house I told you of, and Latour plans to make them sail on that ship. So I overheard him tell the Marquis."

"That's the way of it, eh?" muttered Hatch. "If all these men are agreed with him, he might easily do it."

Jared looked again at the shore near the storehouse, where a dozen or so men were busy; but among them he didn't see Norroy. The schooners were too far distant for him to identify any individual on their decks.

"We must rescue them from Latour before he brings them down to the bay," he said. "There's a man and woman at the house, but I saw no one else. I wanted you and Norroy to help me, but I don't see how I can get word to Norroy. And now the second ship's here, there's no time to lose."

Hatch nodded. "The captain would be like to have his hands full, master, and if you or I ventured out to find him we might be laid by the heels, and afore we could get loose this Latour would have 'em aboard."

"That's how I look at it, Luke. Let's be off then."

Hatch ran his hand down his thigh, a characteristic motion when he scented battle. "I'm with you, Master Lee. Surprise is our game."

Again Jared threaded the woods, and with Hatch crossed the meadow, the second reach of trees, the field beyond, where was the view of the high, wide stretch of ocean, and so reached the pines that bordered the clearing around the dwelling. Here they stopped for a moment, to consider the best plan of approach, and, as fortune had it, almost immediately the man Jared had seen before emerged from the back of the house, a portmanteau in his hand.

"Wait," cautioned Hatch. "Let's see what we have to deal with."

The man set the bag down at the edge of the road and looked over his shoulder.

From the house door came the Marquis and then Jeanne, and close behind them Latour, carrying a small bag.

Hatch laid his hand on Jared's arm. "Wait!" he whispered.

Jared held his pistol gripped in his fingers, and he flung off his friend's hand impatiently.

But at that instant came a voice from the road, its owner hidden from Jared by the clump of pines. "Aha!" cried the voice. "So here we are! Good day to you, Mademoiselle and Monsieur de Severac!"

Into view rode Cornelius Skipworth on a big chestnut mare. He swept off his broad-brimmed beaver hat in an elegant bow, and, much as Jared feared and hated the man, he could not but admit that he made a very gallant figure.

The Marquis's face brightened. As to Jeanne, it seemed to Jared that she paled as she touched her father's sleeve with her finger-tips.

"Were you leaving this charming place?" inquired

Skipworth in a tone he might have used in a drawing-room.

"We're going to the harbor to board the ship that's lately in," said Latour. And added more brusquely, "You know that's how it's been planned."

"Planned?" echoed Skipworth. "I don't know what you're talking about, man!" He lightly vaulted down from his horse. "Do this lady and gentleman desire to go aboard the ship?"

"Decidedly not, sir," said the Marquis, who had now taken his daughter's hand in his and drawn it through his arm.

Latour stepped in front of the couple, his face a sullen red. "I've paid for their passage, as you know. They're in my charge."

Skipworth looked at the Frenchman, and his hooded eye and long nose gave his face that devilishly mocking appearance Jared knew so well. "You seem to be imputing a great deal of knowledge to me, fellow," he said scornfully. "I decline to accept the burden of what you so readily put upon me. If the lady and gentleman don't desire to go aboard the ship I see no reason why they should."

"Mr. Skipworth," spoke up the Marquis, "this man is a great villain. He plans to take us back to France to deliver me up to my enemies; the choice he offers is that or my daughter's marriage to him."

"IF THE LADY AND GENTLEMAN DON'T DESIRE TO GO ABOARD THE SHIP
I SEE NO REASON WHY THEY SHOULD".

The words, quavering a little, were followed by a silence. Then suddenly Latour dropped the bag he had been holding and reached under his coat.

Instantly Skipworth had drawn a pistol and levelled it at the Frenchman. "Hands up!" he ordered.

Latour had no more than obeyed when Skipworth, stepping up to him, pulled the pistol from under his coat and flung it away through the trees. "There," he said, "that will teach you to mind your manners. Put your hands down now, but stand away from me, before I chastise you further." Coolly the elegant gentleman returned his own pistol to his deep coat pocket. "Monsieur de Severac," said he, "what you have just told me plumbs the depths of infamy."

"So *I* thought," agreed the Marquis. "I don't understand how all these events happened, but this man—a neighbor of mine in Normandy and one of the leaders of the mob that attacked my château— managed to overpower at night the driver of the coach which Mr. Mellish had placed at my disposal to take my daughter and me and our servant to Philadelphia. Not being familiar with the roads, it was some time before we became aware of the deception. But we were driven a long distance, by night and day, only stopping occasionally for a change of horses, or when food was thrust in through the coach window; and the route had been carefully chosen, for we drove through no villages, and on our occasional stops we saw only a hostler or pot-boy, and Latour stood at the window, threatening us with his pistol if we raised our voices. My daughter and me he brought here; I do not know what he has done with my servant Sebastien. And this morning he told me his infamous plan."

" 'Tis an unheard of outrage, my dear Monsieur de Severac!" said Skipworth in a tone vibrant with indignation. "What must have been the feelings of your daughter! How fortunate for us all that circumstances brought me in this direction. I was surprised to see you here, but had no thought that it was against your wishes."

Jared knew the man lied. He was convinced that Skipworth, having allowed Latour free rein to bring his plan so near to fulfillment, had assigned to himself the rôle of preserver of the Marquis and Jeanne, a rôle that would certainly place them greatly in his debt.

"How fortunate indeed!" exclaimed the Marquis. "I thank you for my daughter and myself."

Jared looked at Jeanne. She was holding tightly to her father's arm, and her eyes were averted from Skipworth's. The thought came to Jared that, profoundly relieved as she must be at the defeat of Latour's scheme, she would have preferred that any other than Skipworth had been their deliverer.

Skipworth bowed. He knew well how to play his

rôle of gallant rescuer. Then his disposition of the man he had caught in this infamous crime claimed his attention. He stepped back into the road and called to someone at a distance.

In a few minutes a man appeared from the direction of Indian River Bay. To him Skipworth pointed out Latour. "Take that man," he said, "and don't let him out of your sight until I give you further orders in regard to him. Watch him well, for he's a crafty devil." And to Latour Skipworth said, "Go with my man." And to emphasize his command he tapped his coat pocket.

Skipworth's fellow was armed with a stout stick, and with this he pointed out the southward road to the Frenchman, who sullenly did his bidding.

The man who had come out from the house with the portmanteau had gradually been edging toward the trees on the north side of the clearing and now disappeared, leaving the bag at the edge of the road.

Skipworth looked after Latour for a moment, then turned to Jeanne and her father. "I need not tell you, mademoiselle," he said, "how great is my satisfaction at having been able to serve you. For the future I beg you to consider yourself under my special protection." He bowed to the Marquis. "My dearest wish, monsieur, is to serve your daughter."

Jeanne colored. There was an evident point to Skipworth's words that caused her embarrassment.

19

But her father said frankly, "Our debt to you is so great I scarcely know how to repay it."

Skipworth waited, as if hopeful that Jeanne would express herself, but when she still remained silent, with eyes that would not meet his, he smiled and said, "You will be wanting to leave this place at once. If you will walk a short distance with me, I think I can obtain a vehicle of some fashion to take us on our way. I will get the baggage later."

"And Sebastien?" said Jeanne. "What has become of him?"

"Sebastien, of course," assented Skipworth. "I must look for him. But the vehicle first." And he waved his hand toward the road on the north.

Knowing what he did of Skipworth's affairs, Jared trusted him no more than he did Latour. With his pistol pointed at the man he stepped out into the clearing. "Come, Mr. Skipworth," he commanded; "your hands up over your head!"

XXIII

NORROY TAKES A HAND

SKIPWORTH turned, and instantly a smile parted his lips. "On my soul, it's Master Lee!" he exclaimed.

"Your hands over your head!" Jared ordered sternly.

"What a way to speak to an old friend!" Skipworth objected.

But Jared held the pistol levelled and there was a set to his mouth that betokened determination. Still with a smile, made mocking by his heavy-lidded eye, Skipworth raised his hands. "Does that satisfy your lordship?" he inquired sarcastically.

"Luke, take his pistol," directed Jared.

Hatch stalked forward and drew the weapon from Skipworth's coat.

"Now you may put your hands down," said Jared, and lowered his own pistol.

"Thanks, Master Lee," Skipworth responded, accepting the permission. "And to what am I to attribute this pleasantry on your part?"

"Yes," broke in the Marquis de Severac, "I don't understand the gentleman's behavior."

291

Jared glanced at Jeanne, and something in her eyes told him that she, at least, appreciated his action.

"I prefer," he said, "that when the Marquis and his daughter leave this place they do so under my escort. I think they will be safer that way."

"Indeed!" exclaimed Skipworth, amusement in his tone and look, as though he were much entertained at a comedy he was watching.

The Marquis, however, shook his head at the young fellow, who, with his rustic companion, had so unexpectedly appeared and behaved in such an arbitrary manner. "You are not familiar with the circumstances, Mr. Lee," he remonstrated. "This gentleman has done me a very great service."

"I beg your pardon, monsieur," said Jared, "but I think I am familiar with all the circumstances. I saw what took place here. But from what I have learned in various ways I'm convinced that Mr. Skipworth is not to be trusted. How comes he to be here, on this southern coast of Delaware, with a man —and more than one man, most likely—at his beck and call? He has his own purpose to serve, monsieur; and that's why I insist on escorting Mademoiselle Jeanne and you myself, without any assistance from him."

Skipworth smiled. "And how comes Master Lee to be here, with a man at *his* beck and call? One would think to hear him talk that he was the only honest man in the world."

At that Jared grew hot, for there was always something about Skipworth that had the power to sting him. "I am here," he said, looking at Jeanne, "because when you didn't arrive in Philadelphia on the day you were expected I rode to Mr. Mellish's for information. I found the tavern where you stopped for supper, and from what I learned there I thought you had been deceived. I came down to this part of the country hunting for you. And I know that Mr. Skipworth is in league with a band of pirates off the Delaware Capes."

"Impossible!" exclaimed the Marquis. But Jeanne, her hand on her father's arm, looked at him and said, "I had much rather we went with Mr. Lee."

"I assure you I know this country much better than he does, mademoiselle," said Skipworth. "It is true that I have a number of men here with me. And should Master Lee fall in with these pirates, as he calls them, his escort might not prove so serviceable as he boasts." Skipworth glanced at the Marquis. "You understand the situation better than your daughter, monsieur."

Jared appreciated that Skipworth unquestionably knew the neighboring country and that every moment of delay might bring some of the men from

Indian River Bay to the latter's aid. He must get his friends away, and trust to being able to find some conveyance for them. But what should he do with Skipworth? The only answer seemed to be to bind him and leave him in the woods.

"Luke," said Jared, "find me a piece of rope. I'm obliged to make sure Mr. Skipworth doesn't give us any trouble."

"Have a care, Master Lee!" Skipworth's cheeks flushed.

"Indeed sir," said the Marquis, "I can't see the gentleman treated so!"

"I regret the necessity, monsieur," Jared answered, his face red, but determined. "Luke, there must be rope in the house."

Hatch went to the back door and into the dwelling. Skipworth, his eyes on the face of the Marquis, said, "I thought this was a matter to be discussed between gentlemen; but it seems I was mistaken. If I'm to be treated as a felon—"

"Mr. Lee," interrupted the Marquis, disengaging Jeanne's hand from his arm and stepping toward Jared; "Mr. Skipworth has been a guest at Bellevue, an intimate friend of Mr. Mellish. That in itself should be a guarantee of his honor."

Here, however, Jeanne intervened. "I think that Mr. Lee may be better informed than we are. Please don't oppose him."

Jared flashed her a look of thanks. At the same moment Skipworth, glancing around him, took stock of the situation. His horse, busily engaged in cropping the green herbage, had strayed too far for him to spring to the saddle and be off on her back. But as he looked down the road toward Indian River Bay he saw something that gave him confidence. He turned again to the Marquis. " 'Tis idle to speak of the usages of gentlemen to such as Master Lee," he declared.

Jared stifled a hot retort. "Can't you find a rope, Luke?" he called.

"Aye, master, here is one," said Hatch, coming out at the door.

"Bind his hands," ordered Jared.

With a curl to his lips that was half smile, half sneer Skipworth held out his arms. Hatch handed Jared the pistol he had taken from Skipworth and walked toward their prisoner.

Before he reached him, however, Skipworth sprang back to the road. "Fire, Master Lee!" he cried. "I'll not be tied up like a fowl!"

To fire point-blank at an unarmed man was more than Jared could do, as Skipworth had conjectured. He dropped one pistol and started forward, as did Hatch, to catch the man before he could reach his horse.

From the road to the south came a loud voice. "What's all this? Stop where you are!"

Skipworth stopped, as if the voice had been a bullet that had struck him. Then he turned toward his chestnut mare, but that wise beast, as if scenting some danger, had taken to her heels.

The next instant Norroy came into view, running. He reached the clearing and halted.

"Ah, Cornelius!" he exclaimed. "Well met! I've been hoping to find you!" His eyes swept the group. "And here are Monsieur and Mademoiselle de Severac, Master Jared and the good Hatch."

"You come at an opportune moment, Hal," said Skipworth. "Perhaps *you* can teach this cub of a law student the manners of a gentleman. Monsieur de Severac and I have tried, but he's difficult at learning."

"Indeed!" answered Norroy, lifting surprised eyebrows. "Monsieur le Marquis, do you also find Master Jared so unmannered?"

"He is somewhat arbitrary, I must confess," said the Marquis. "I do not understand him."

"But I do, Mr. Norroy." It was Jeanne who spoke, eagerness in her voice. "He doesn't trust Mr. Skipworth. But I trust Mr. Lee."

Norroy smiled at her; then his eyes shifted to Jared.

"At least you have the lady on your side, Jared,"

he observed. "But how does it happen that you don't trust Cornelius?"

"Mr. Skipworth has saved us from peril," put in the Marquis. "He has rescued us from a villain who was going to take us to France."

"That is so," said Jared. "But I don't trust Skipworth. I'm not willing to let them go with him."

"He thinks his escort safer than mine," sneered Skipworth. "I pointed out to him that he knows nothing of this part of the country, while I know it well. In spite of that he was going to bind me, and himself lead the Marquis and his daughter through the wilderness. The fool! He'd have got into trouble before he'd gone a mile!"

"You do seem to have shouldered considerable responsibility, Jared," said Norroy. "But perhaps you don't know as much about Cornelius as he and I know concerning him."

"I know enough about him," was Jared's short retort. "I know he's not to be trusted."

"That's a lie," said Skipworth.

Jared's hand clenched and he took a step forward.

"No, no," Norroy interposed, striding between the two. "As Cornelius said, it does appear that I've come at an opportune moment. I comprehend the situation better than any one else. Cornelius and I have seen a good deal of each other—intimately. That is so, isn't it?"

Skipworth nodded.

"And I know just how far he is to be trusted," Norroy continued. "And that is—not at all."

"Eh?" said Skipworth, as if he didn't understand.

"Admitting for the sake of argument that he and I have both been breakers of the law," Norroy went on, "there is still such a thing as honor among thieves. Cornelius, however, forgot that. He planned to stab me in the back."

"What's the jest, Hal?" said Skipworth, frowning down his nose.

"There is no jest." And suddenly as a cloud obscures the sun and chills the landscape the humor vanished from Norroy's face and voice and was replaced by a cold and biting anger. "You plotted with my mate Rand to destroy me. And it was your evil scheming that brought this innocent gentleman and his daughter to this wretched place. Trust you? I'd rather trust a snake!"

Skipworth's face was livid. Hate of the man before him glittered in his eyes. Wordless, he sprang at Norroy, and so swift and impetuous was his leap that he almost sent his enemy reeling by the impact.

The two men twisted and turned, each fighting for a footing, for a purchase against the other. Then

Norroy crooked his knee, caught his leg inside that of Skipworth, and with a sudden lurch sent the other flying backward.

Skipworth lay in the road, and above him stood Norroy, vengeful of face.

Jared found a hand trembling on his arm, and looked down at Jeanne.

"Maybe I'd better bind him now, Master Lee," said Hatch, who still held the rope.

Jared nodded. He was occupied at the moment in taking Jeanne's hand and holding it tight in a reassuring grip.

Norroy turned from Skipworth, and, his hands on his hips, rested for a few minutes. Then he said to the Marquis, "Jared was right, monsieur. I will explain all this to you later. But you must be fatigued, and so must be your daughter. I suggest that we go into the house. Hatch will attend to Skipworth."

XXIV

THE GENTLEMAN-ADVENTURER

THE Marquis was indeed in an amazement at the events that had trod so closely one upon another's heels, and in which in turn Latour, Skipworth, Jared Lee, and Norroy had each played a principal part. He was also considerably fatigued by the warmth of the summer day, and as soon as he had gone in at the rear door of the house and so come into the kitchen he sat down on a settle and applied his handkerchief to his heated face. Jeanne, who was herself scarcely less amazed at the adventures of the past half-hour, found a jug of water and pouring some into a cup gave it to her father to drink. Then she sat down beside him. For the first time in many days she felt free from worry.

"Who lives in this house?" asked Norroy, standing in the kitchen.

"There's a man and a woman," Jeanne answered. "The man went up the road while we were talking outside."

Norroy stepped into the front hall and called in a loud voice, "Woman, come here at once! Nobody's going to harm you."

After a minute the woman in the calico dress came

doubtfully down the stairs. "What do you want, sir?" she asked, eyeing the stranger.

"Food," said Norroy. "The best you have that you can serve quickly, and a jug of cool water. I'll pay you well for it."

In the kitchen, while the woman busied herself setting out cold viands, Norroy explained his desire for refreshment. "I haven't eaten since dawn," he said, "and it's now past noon. I've had my hands full this day, and there's more work to be done. And since I have to wait here for several men, I thought mademoiselle wouldn't object if I had a bite of dinner. Possibly I might persuade her and her father and Jared to join me."

"I think we might," smiled Jeanne. "My father and I have had but poor appetites up to now."

"And I haven't had anything since breakfast," said Jared, "and that seems weeks ago."

The woman of the house fetched a jug of cool water from the well and furnished the kitchen table with meat and bread and vegetables. Assured by Norroy that they could eat without danger of interruption the other three followed his example and made a good meal.

When Norroy had finished he went out, saw that Skipworth was safely secured by the rope to a tree at the edge of the clearing, and returned to the

house with Hatch. While Hatch ate his dinner
Norroy addressed himself to the Marquis and Jeanne.

"Jared was entirely in the right," he said, "and
when it comes to giving thanks for your deliverance,
monsieur, you owe them all to him. Master Lee is
one of the few altogether honorable men you have
yet met in this country. He is a student of the law,
and the rest of us, including even the excellent
Joshua Mellish, have devoted ourselves to the study
of how we might most profitably break it."

"You amaze me, sir!" said the Marquis, who,
since he had rested and eaten, felt a great desire
to get to the bottom of this extraordinary situation.
"The men I met at Mr. Mellish's all appeared to
be gentlemen."

Norroy smiled. "Fine feathers don't always make
fine birds, monsieur. I have known great noblemen
in Europe, whose dress and manners were above
reproach, who were no better as to morals than
the lowest thieves in the kennels, not so good indeed,
for the noblemen didn't want for food, and the
thieves usually did. However, that is not important.
Cornelius Skipworth has played the part of highwayman, as I have once or twice. None of Mr. Mellish's
guests have been inconvenienced by us—except Jared
on one occasion—the highwaymen have devoted
themselves to relieving fat farmers of some of their
surplus wealth, as in the case of the two brothers

whom Jared pointed out to me one night at the
tavern in Philadelphia, and whom I had met on the
road earlier that evening when I lightened their load.
Cornelius, in addition, was the purveyor of information concerning cargoes outward bound from the
city and an adept in the means of disposing of those
cargoes after they were secured. I know all this,
monsieur, because I have commanded the ship that
captured the prizes."

"You, Mr. Norroy!" exclaimed Jeanne, unbelief
in her blue eyes.

"Impossible, sir!" said the Marquis. "You ask
me to believe that you are—no better than a pirate?"

"Jared can tell you," said Norroy. "He has been
aboard my ship; he has seen her in action. He
didn't ship as one of the crew, but to save me
from Skipworth and Rand."

Two pairs of eyes turned to Jared, who, vastly
uncomfortable, could only stare back at them.

"You see," said Norroy. "Well, I make no excuses. But I've left the ship today, and shall never
set foot on her again."

There was a resounding sound, as of a broad palm
striking a stalwart thigh, and Norroy shifted his
glance to Hatch, who still sat at the kitchen table.
"I'm glad to hear it, sir!" said the sturdy country-
man. "The little taste I had of that ship cured me
of any liking for sea-faring."

Norroy laughed; here was an opportunity to lighten the situation. "You were not patterned for a buccaneer, were you, Hatch? No, I don't think you were, nor Jared either. And yet it takes all stripes of men to make up a world, even a world of buccaneers." His gaze rounded to Jared, and there was a note of extenuation in his voice, as if to Jared alone he felt that he owed an apology. "Whatever I may do, the Philadelphia merchants sha'n't suffer from me again. Before I left the schooner I had a talk with the crew. Roach and most of the men are sailing for the Barbadoes; they will take Rand and the other two prisoners with them and set them free at some port in the West Indies. That's better than the scamps deserve." He shrugged his shoulders. "I didn't want to hang them."

Jared nodded. He felt that he understood Norroy, this new Norroy at least, who was so much like the man he had earlier admired.

"A few of the men are leaving the schooner," Norroy continued, "and going with me. As soon as they get here we will find some conveyance to take the Marquis and Mademoiselle to Philadelphia."

"But where is our servant, Sebastien?" asked Jeanne. "We must find him."

"He's at the storehouse on the bay," said Norroy, "and my men will bring him here. I found him a prisoner there when I went ashore. I was talking to him when one of the men came in with Latour. That was how I learned that Skipworth was in the neighborhood. I was particularly desirous of encountering Cornelius." He smiled and bowed to Jeanne. "As well as eager to renew my acquaintance with Mademoiselle de Severac and her father."

"What will you do with him now?" asked Jared.

"I think a sea voyage will benefit his health," Norroy answered. "I shall send him to accompany Latour on the schooner. I judge that neither of them would find Philadelphia a pleasant hunting-ground after you return."

With that he rose. "Ah, well, Jared," he said, his eyes on those of his friend, "I've made the best amends I could for what must seem to you a sorry business. If it were possible I would restore the cargo of this latest prize to its rightful owners, but that is out of my power. The crew would not allow it."

Again Jared nodded, while Jeanne and the Marquis regarded with mixed sentiments this extraordinary man, a gentleman—for such he undoubtedly was in the common acceptance of that term—who had also been a pirate, according to his own admission.

"Here comes Sebastien now," said Norroy, looking through the open door.

Jeanne ran from the house to meet the gray-haired man, who exclaimed with delight at the sight of

20

his dear mistress. After her came the Marquis and the three talked together while Norroy directed two of the men who had come with Sebastien to take Cornelius Skipworth back to Indian River Bay and give him in charge of Roach.

Another man he sent, provided with money, to find a conveyance that should take them to Lewes. By the middle of the afternoon the man was back with a farmer, who drove a pair of horses harnessed to a wide, two-seated wagon that swung on leather bands.

Meantime Hatch, searching along the road to the north, had come upon Skipworth's chestnut mare, and brought her back. Norroy leapt into the saddle. Jared helped Jeanne and her father to the rear seat of the wagon and took his place beside them; Sebastien climbed up by the driver. And as the wagon and the horseman started off north back of them came Hatch and four of Norroy's crew, stalwart rogues, as ready to follow their leader ashore as they had been to do his bidding on board the schooner.

It was dusk when they came into Lewes and drew up at the small tavern, which was the only public-house the village provided. Norroy paid off the farmer. The innkeeper took the bags of the Marquis and Jeanne to their chambers abovestairs, and found a third room for Norroy and Jared.

The four guests had the dining-room to themselves, and sat for some time at table after supper was finished, for each had much to tell. Still the Marquis found it difficult to believe that he, at Mellish's house, had been surrounded by a network of intrigue. To Jeanne the discovery was not so astonishing; from the first she had had her doubts concerning the too-genial owner of Bellevue, and for Skipworth she had felt positive antipathy.

Next morning a chaise was procured to take them to Milford. Norroy had a talk with his men, the four who had come with Hatch to Lewes and the two who had taken Skipworth to Indian River Bay and who had now rejoined the party; he arranged with them to meet him in Lewes again in a few days. Hatch was afoot early, and when the chaise arrived at the Inn of the Three Pigeons there he was in the road with Jared's horse and his own. Luckily for the innkeeper he had taken good care of the two steeds, for Hatch had sworn dire punishment on the shifty-eyed man if he had ill-treated their mounts.

Jared didn't ask the innkeeper if he had looked into their room the night they had spent at his house; the man would of course have denied it, and no harm had come from such spying anyhow.

The Delaware countryside was at its fairest, and travel was a delight as they went north by roads along the river. There was no need for haste, and they made the journey by comfortable stages, changing carriages and horses frequently and resting when they chose. Jeanne, to whom the recent days had been like a nightmare, bloomed with happiness at being again among friends, and laughed with Norroy and Jared, who rode for much of the time alongside the chaise. Norroy was as nimble-tongued as ever, and always gallant in the presence of beauty; and Jared, though he talked less, and frequently was content for long stretches to listen to the light chatter of the other two without taking part in it, enjoyed every mile of the journey.

They spent a night at Dover and another at New Castle, and on the following day came into the country near Mr. Mellish's. They did not turn aside at Bellevue, however, Jared's first concern being to get his friends safely to the city. At the farmstead near the crossroads they separated from Hatch. The Marquis and Jeanne pressed his hand and thanked him warmly for all he had done on their behalf. "I shall ride out to see you soon, Luke," said Jared; "and when you come to Philadelphia you shall have the best welcome the city can provide."

Norroy also shook Hatch's hand. "I never forget a shipmate," he said; "least of all such a stout-fighting one as you. Good luck to you in your battles!"

Hatch muttered something incoherent, and as the

chaise and the two horsemen drew away he stood for some moments staring after them, still puzzled by the inconsistency of a gentleman who had been a pirate.

Late in the afternoon they came to the broad stretch where the waters of the Schuylkill flow into the Delaware, and turned aside to the ferry. As the chaise stopped Norroy and Jared dismounted. Norroy, his hat in his hand, approached the carriage. "Here I will say farewell, mademoiselle," he declared. "If you can find it in your heart to do so, I beg you to remember me sometimes in your prayers. The prayers of such a sweet lady should avail me something if anything can, hardened sinner that I am."

There was a mist in Jeanne's blue eyes as she looked at the tall, graceful man who, even in his penitence, still wore an impenitent air. Doubtless there were excuses to be made for him, did she but know all his story. Certainly he had done all in his power to befriend herself and her father. She held out her hand and permitted him to raise it to his lips.

"Goodby, Mr. Norroy. I shall remember you in my prayers. And, oh, may you be happy!"

He smiled. "Happy? Ah, yes, I shall still search for the pot of gold at the foot of the rainbow." Gently he released her hand, and turned to the

Marquis. "I am not an American, monsieur," he said, "but I beg of you not to think too ill of this country because of what you have seen so far of its people. You have only known a few of them, and I have known a great many; and most of them are fine and honorable and kindly." He put his hand on the arm of Jared, who had come up to him. "Honorable and kindly, like Jared Lee," he added.

Then with a quick movement he slid his hand down Jared's arm until he grasped the young man's fingers. "Goodby, my boy," he said. "I shall ride back to Lewes, and pick up my band of men. We shall disappear in the forest. Stick to your last, my lad. There are worse fates than becoming Lord Chief Justice or even a respectable citizen like Nathaniel Carroll."

"But Hal," urged Jared, "you'll let me hear from you sometime?"

For a moment Norroy looked deep into his friend's eyes. "I shall want to, Jared," he answered; "but even if I never do, I think you will understand."

Lightly he stepped to his horse and swung himself up to the saddle. A wave of his hat and he was off, riding south along the road by which they had just travelled.

The city was bathed in gold as the De Severacs and Jared rode through the leafy streets. The quiet of the summer twilight was on the people they passed, and the substantial houses, with their flower-filled gardens, seemed the abode of peace. To Fourth and Prune Streets they went and stopped before the wide door of Mr. Carroll's mansion.

Jared jumped down to the footway. From the door, now open, came an excited voice, Hannah's: "Why, I declare, it's Jared with the French people!"

Down the path Hannah ran, and after her Elizabeth. Before they reached the chaise Mr. and Mrs. Carroll stood in the doorway.

"We only stopped for a moment," Jared said to the sisters. "We're going on to Mrs. Derbyshire's."

"Nonsense, Jared Lee!" retorted Hannah. "You're all coming right in to supper. Here we've been thinking all kinds of dreadful things must have happened to you. You've got to tell us what you've been doing. Do come in, mademoiselle!" she entreated Jeanne.

"Of course they will," boomed the deep voice of Mr. Carroll over Hannah's shoulder. "If you will kindly step out of my way, my dear Hannah, I will assist Mademoiselle de Severac and her father to alight."

As she entered the wide, cool hall, with Mrs. Carroll's arm slipped through hers, Jeanne gave a sigh of content. It was very pleasant to be in a civilized house again, and moreover a house in which there were gentlewomen. She felt as if for some time now her world had been peopled almost exclusively by men.

XXV

THE REFUGEES AMONG FRIENDS

THE story that Jared Lee told the Carrolls that evening was known through the length and breadth of Philadelphia by the next sunset. Nathaniel Carroll himself took the story to the court-house in the morning, from whence it spread to offices, shops and warehouses along the river. Mrs. Carroll related it to her most intimate friends before she went to market. Elizabeth and Hannah hurried from breakfast to make a round of all the girls they knew, to whom they narrated Jared's recital with embellishments of their own. By noon the story was being discussed on street corners; by nightfall it was the sole topic of conversation in the city's homes.

Mr. Carroll held a conference with the leading merchants, at which Jared was present, and the subject was studied from every angle. But, if Jared's story were to be believed, the pirates had left the Delaware Capes and were now out of reach. Thereupon it was voted to take action and send a party of men to scour the coast from the Schuylkill to Indian River Bay. This was done, and everything was found as Jared had described, but all the birds of prey had flown.

Norroy was out of reach, for which Jared was greatly thankful. Skipworth was a prisoner on the schooner bound for the Barbadoes. Jared was curious as to Joshua Mellish, and on an early day he took the south road, with which he was now so familiar, and stopping for Luke Hatch, went with him to Bellevue.

The country place was as beautiful as ever, a bower of lustrous green, but the stable yard was empty, and when they knocked on the front door of the mansion no one answered the summons.

Stepping back to the driveway the two looked up at the house. "It's empty, master," said Hatch. "Mr. Mellish has gone away."

Jared nodded. He was not surprised. "I think he'd have found it awkward to answer some of the questions that people would have been asking him. What an odd character, Luke—with his passion for entertaining; there was a real friendliness about him; and yet I very much doubt if his money was legally come by."

Mellish had disappeared, and this to Mr. Carroll was sufficient evidence of his guilt. The lawyer frequently discussed the owner of Bellevue with the Marquis de Severac over their Madeira, and the French gentleman continued to protest that he found it impossible to believe that his former host—so courteous and so hospitable—was actually a reprobate. This view, however, as Mr. Carroll pointed out to Jared when they were alone, was that of a man of a simple, confiding nature, one who had never had occasion to study the characters of men but was satisfied to believe that such as spoke him fairly were as honorable as he.

At one time the name of Norroy was mentioned in conversation between the lawyer and his student and Jared took the occasion to tell Mr. Carroll the few incidents he knew concerning his friend's early life. "I believe he is an English nobleman," he said, "who was early left an orphan and was brought up without any guidance or care. He sympathized with the under-dog, and some acts of injustice that he learned of made him hate the law. He helped some poor thief to escape the gallows, and for this he had to fly the country. And the love of adventure is stronger in him than anything else."

Mr. Carroll took a pinch of snuff, and for several minutes was silent. "I know you admire many things about this man, Jared," he said, "and I am willing to concede that, since you find certain good qualities in him, he may not be as wicked as he seems. But Norroy is a man of intelligence; and for what is intelligence given to us unless to avoid evil?"

"If he had been started right I think he would have been a splendid man," said Jared.

"Possibly," answered Mr. Carroll. "But that is an argument that is scarcely admissible in either a court of law or a court of morals. No, Jared, my boy, as a man who has spent many years in trying to distinguish right from wrong I cannot see this Norroy in any other light than that of a wilful law-breaker."

Jared said nothing more. He knew that no words of his could make Nathaniel Carroll see Norroy as he saw him. He was even willing to admit that his own view of Norroy might be wildly quixotic. But something in the character and the charm of that undisciplined, adventurous character had so seized on his affection that he knew that to him Norroy the pirate would always seem Norroy the friend.

In this feeling he was, to a certain degree, supported by Jeanne. She saw the man more clearly than Jared did, and sometimes smilingly shook her head when he spoke too admiringly of him. "I think he is a man," she said, "who, in spite of his wayward acts, would always be honorable toward women. I would trust him, Jared. And I think you could trust him. But as to moral scruples in other directions"—she shrugged her shoulders; "the less said the better."

Jared understood, and admitted that her judgment was right. He felt, moreover, that she appreciated, and did not criticize, his own feeling toward his friend.

Of the Marquis and his daughter Jared saw a great deal, asserting that it was his business to see that no harm came to them in the city. When he said this in Hannah's presence she always stuck out the tip of her tongue at him, and if neither of the French people was present she was apt to remark, "Business indeed, Master Jared! What devotion to business you have!"

But though Hannah liked to tease him about Jeanne, she greatly approved of the French girl. As soon as the De Severacs were established in rooms at Mrs. Derbyshire's Jeanne began to give lessons in her native tongue, and, thanks to Mrs. Carroll, found plenty of pupils. Twice a week she went to Mrs. Carroll's house, where she instructed a number of ladies in the niceties of French conversation. And so much did Elizabeth and Hannah enjoy her society that they were constantly finding excuses to visit Mrs. Derbyshire's.

August of that year, however, brought the grievous yellow plague to the city, and all who could do so left. The Carrolls went out to Germantown, where Mrs. Carroll's brother lived. Jared rode to Lancaster and had a talk with his parents, and when

he returned to Philadelphia he brought a letter to
the Marquis, inviting him and his daughter to make
the Lees a visit.

In the capacious country house, looking out over
Mr. Lee's broad acres, the old nobleman felt very
much at home. Jeanne became the companion of
Jared and his brothers and sisters, a lively family,
and the capable helper of Mrs. Lee in her needle-
work and many domestic duties. An only child, she
greatly enjoyed a house full of young people, and the
reserve she had felt compelled to assume while at
Bellevue vanished before the simple hospitality of
these kind, unselfish friends.

It was November before the city was rid of the
plague. On a cool and windy morning Jeanne and
her father and Sebastien, with Jared said farewell
to the Lees and set out in the coach for Philadelphia.
Arrived there, the French people went to Mrs.
Derbyshire's and Jared to Mrs. Bird's. The next
morning Jared reported at Mr. Carroll's office and
took up his law studies with uncommon zeal.

He had a goal now in view, and ambition set
spurs to his labor. Mr. Carroll, observing how
much more industrious and eager his student was this
winter than in the year before, smiled to himself
and found opportunities to provide Jared with work
that would bring him some money.

By spring Jared was a lawyer. Meantime Jeanne,

by her teaching, earned enough to support her father and herself. Sebastien was employed for part of his time in housework and gardening by the Carrolls and their friends, the rest of it he devoted to the service of his master.

A second year rolled around, and Jared was taking care of the legal business of some of Mr. Carroll's clients. And that June, when the spell of adventure was again in the air and the trees and gardens of the town were in bloom, a little group met at the church on Fourth Street for a wedding service. The Marquis de Severac gave the bride away, a very lovely bride with eyes as blue as the sea, and Jared slipped the ring on Jeanne's finger. The bride and groom walked down from the altar and stood for a moment at the door of the church.

"Jared, my dear husband," whispered Jeanne, "how glad I am that I came from France!"

"Not half so glad as I am, dearest!" said Jared. "But if you hadn't I'd have gone to France and further to find and bring you here."

THE END